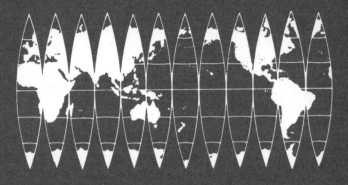

Editor in Chief • PHILLIP BACON

Professor of Geography
Teachers College, Columbia University

Managing Editor • JOANNA ALDENDORFF

Picture Researcher • PETER J. GALLAGHER

Associate Editor • PETER R. LIMBURG

Cartographer • VINCENT KOTSCHAR

Picture Editor • ROBERT J. GARLOCK

Designer • FRANCES GIANNONI

Staff • JUDY KORMAN, BARBARA VINSON, KATHLEEN SEAGRAVES, JOHANNA GREENWALD

Special Section of Statistical Maps • RICHARD EDES HARRISON

Covers • RAY PIOCH

Complete List of Books

These books tell the exciting story of how people live in all parts of the world. You will see how men use the land for farming and industry. You will learn about mountains and deserts, oceans and rivers, cities and towns—and you will discover how the daily life of people in other countries compares with your own.

BOOK 1 • NORTH AMERICA

BOOK 2 • SOUTH AMERICA

BOOK 3 • EUROPE

BOOK 4 • ASIA

BOOK 5 • AFRICA

BOOK 6 • AUSTRALIA, OCEANIA
AND THE POLAR LANDS

WITH A SPECIAL SECTION OF
STATISTICAL MAPS AND INDEX

BOOK 2

SOUTH AMERICA

BY MARGARET BEVANS

THE GOLDEN BOOK

PICTURE ATLAS

OF THE WORLD

IN SIX VOLUMES

Illustrated with More than 1,000 Color Photographs and Maps

GOLDEN PRESS · NEW YORK

© COPYRIGHT 1960 BY GOLDEN PRESS, INC. DESIGNED AND PRODUCED BY ARTISTS AND WRITERS PRESS, INC. PRINTED IN THE U.S.A. BY WESTERN PRINTING AND LITHOGRAPHING COMPANY. PUBLISHED BY GOLDEN PRESS, INC., ROCKEFELLER CENTER, NEW YORK 20, N. Y.

Erwin Verity

The Andes are new mountains, still sharp and very high. The chain runs all the way down the west coast.

THIS IS SOUTH AMERICA

The South American continent reaches from the Caribbean Sea in the north almost to the Antarctic continent in the south. With the Atlantic Ocean on the east and the Pacific on the west, South America is almost completely surrounded by water. Its only connection with another continent is a narrow strip of land, the Isthmus of Panama, which links it to North America.

South America is nearly 5,000 miles long from north to south, and 3,100 miles wide from east to west. The continent has an area of almost seven million square miles—over twice the size of the United States without Alaska, and about one seventh of the total land area of the world. There are about 130,000,000 people in South America—a little more than two thirds of the population of the United States.

Many people think of South America as being directly south of the United States. Actually, it is far to the east. If you drew a line straight south from New York City, more than nine tenths of South America would be east of it.

People who are not well acquainted with South America sometimes think all its countries are alike. But they are very different from each other in terrain, climate, people, and natural resources.

There are ten republics in South America: Argentina, Bolivia, Brazil, Chile, Colombia, Ecuador, Paraguay, Peru, Uruguay, and Venezuela. There are also three European colonies: British Guiana, French Guiana, and Surinam, or Dutch Guiana.

If you looked at a relief model of South America, you would see that a great chain of mountains, the Andes, runs all the way down the western edge of the continent. In the north and east of the continent are two other highland areas. There are also three great river systems with vast lowland areas in their valleys.

The Andes are the longest continuous mountain barrier in the world. They run like a towering wall for four thousand miles, from the Caribbean Sea in the north to the tip of Tierra del Fuego in the south. They are the second highest mountains in the world (only the Himalayas are higher).

SOUTH AMERICA

Scale 1:30,000,000

| | 0 | 100 | 200 | 300 | 400 | 500 Miles |

SAO PAULO   *Cities over*   1,000,000 *population*
Barranquilla   *Cities of 250,000 —* 1,000,000 *population*
Puerto Montt   *Cities under*   250,000 *population*
     ⊙ *Capitals of Countries*

Depths in feet: Heights in feet:

| over 650 | 0-650 | | Below sea level | 0-650 | 650-1650 | 1650-4900 | over 4900 |

― Railroads   ⊥ Canals   ↓ Head of navigation   ⚡ Falls
    Salt lake   Swamp marsh

Hugh A. Wilmar

Many Andean volcanoes are still active. Their slopes are covered with ash from their craters.

wide plateaus and valleys whose bottoms may be over two miles above sea level.

Although the Andes were heaved up from the bottom of the sea millions of years ago, there are signs that the earth's crust is still shifting here. Some of the mountains are active volcanoes, outlets for molten rock from far beneath the earth's surface. And there are many earthquakes along the west coast and in the mountains. The Andes are what geologists call "young" mountains. They are high and rugged.

The two other highland areas — the Guiana Highlands in the northeast and the Brazilian Highlands in the eastern bulge of the continent — are geologically "ancient" formations. The rocks of which they are composed are very old. Some of the mountains here rise as high as 9,000 feet, but they are not sharp, crested peaks like the Andes. They have been worn down by natural forces until they are flat-topped or rounded. But their slopes are steep.

Several of the peaks are over 21,000 feet high, and Mt. Aconcagua, the highest, reaches 22,835 feet.

At their widest point, in Bolivia, the Andes are four hundred miles wide. In most places they are about a hundred and fifty miles wide. The chain of mountains spreads out into fingers, especially in the north. Between these fingers are deep valleys. Higher in the mountains there are

The Guiana Highlands lie in Venezuela, the three Guianas, and northern Brazil. They are almost unoccupied because the land is so rugged and hard to reach.

Chile's Atacama Desert is one of the driest places on earth, but much of it was once lake bottom.

Eric Pavel—FLO

The Brazilian Highlands begin south of the Amazon River. They cover a much larger area than the Guiana Highlands, which they are otherwise very like. The Brazilian Highlands are highest along the east coast of Brazil, which is rugged, with many natural harbors. The eastern portion of the highlands has rich soil and is forested. Most of Brazil's people live here. The western portion, where few people live, is grassland. The highland slopes down by step-like terraces to the valleys of the Amazon in the north and the Paraná and Paraguay rivers in the west and south.

The west coast of South America is a forbidding place for most of its length. Much of it is made up of great, rocky cliffs which rise straight out of the ocean. One of the world's most barren deserts runs along the coast for a thousand miles, from southern Ecuador to northern Chile. There are few lowlands. The region is one of plateaus and mountains. The coastline is so straight that there are very few harbors except in the north and south.

East of the Andes and south of the Brazilian highlands is a high plateau. In southern Argentina this plateau, here called Patagonia, reaches all the way to the east coast. Several rivers travel across the plateau. In many of the valleys there are lakes formed by the glaciers of the ice age, which dumped huge masses of material ground off the mountains and created dams. Except for the oases around the rivers and lakes, much of this southern plateau is barren.

In the far south, the west coast has been worn down and broken into fiords and islands by glaciers and pounding seas. The mountains are lower here than in the north, but they are still high enough to protect the eastern side of the mountains from the constant rain and storms.

South America has three great rivers: the Orinoco, the Amazon, and the Paraná-Paraguay system.

The Orinoco rises in the Guiana Highlands on the Venezuelan-Brazilian border. It flows in a great semicircle northwest, north, and east, emptying into the Atlantic Ocean through a wide delta. Some of its tributaries rise in the Andes. The Orinoco is about 1,800 miles long and is navigable

The winding Amazon River flows over 2,000 miles through lowlands covered with dense rainforest.

H. Noodt

Courtesy of PANAGRA

Lake Titicaca is over 12,000 feet high. The Aymara Indians make their rafts of woven reeds.

for about 1,000 miles of its length. There is a large lowland area along its middle and lower course.

The Amazon is the second longest river in the world. With its tributaries, it drains at least half of the South American continent. Its hot, steamy plain varies from twenty to eight hundred miles in width; for most of its length the plain is about fifty miles wide.

The Amazon's headwaters rise in the Andes, about one hundred miles from the Pacific Ocean. Its tributaries come from the Andes, the Brazilian Highlands, and the Guiana highlands.

The Amazon itself is about 4,000 miles long. Together with its tributaries, it has about 5,600 miles of water navigable by shallow-draft boats. Ocean-going ships can go upstream as far as Manaus, around 1,000 miles from the mouth, and vessels with a 14-foot draft can go as far as Iquitos, in Peru, approximately 2,300 miles from the sea.

Brazil's Iguassú River drops 210 feet into a gorge in a spectacular waterfall two and a half miles wide.

Wolfe Worldwide Films, Los Angeles 24, Calif.

The Amazon carries so much water from the highlands into the ocean that the water is fresh on the surface of the sea for forty miles beyond the mouth of the river. So much silt is carried by the river that the ocean is muddy for two hundred miles out.

The Paraná and Paraguay rivers drain the southern portion of the Brazilian Highlands and the central Andes. Their valley forms South America's third great lowland.

Many of the Brazilian tributaries rise in the highest part of the Brazilian Highland, which is just behind Rio de Janeiro and São Paulo on the east coast. Here the slope of the land is such that most of the rivers flow away from the coast toward the Paraná-Paraguay plain. They have cut deep, gorge-like valleys in the plateau.

The northern part of the Paraná-Paraguay plain is an almost empty area of wooded grasslands called the *Gran Chaco,* an almost flat plain sloping from the Andes to the Paraguay River. In the south is a vast, fertile, level area called the Humid Pampa. The Humid Pampa, which lies in Argentina, is South America's biggest cattle-raising and grain-producing region.

Hallingsworth—Black Star

The mountains of stormy southern Patagonia are covered with glaciers descending to icy lakes.

The Paraná River empties into the sea through a gigantic estuary called the Río de la Plata. The Plata, 170 miles long and 140 miles wide at its mouth, is more like an enormous bay than a river.

There are a number of lakes in South America, but few of them are large. The largest lakes are Lake Maracaibo, in Venezuela, Lake Titicaca, between Bolivia and Peru, and salty Lake Poopó, in Bolivia.

Windswept Tierra del Fuego is separated from the southern tip of South America by the Strait of Magellan.

Fritz Hack

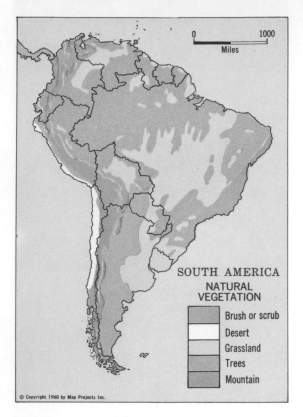

SOUTH AMERICA
NATURAL
VEGETATION

- Brush or scrub
- Desert
- Grassland
- Trees
- Mountain

© Copyright 1960 by Map Projects Inc.

The Galápagos Islands, 650 miles west of Ecuador in the Pacific, are famous for their giant tortoises.

South America is like North America in having worn-down mountains in the east and more rugged mountains in the west. But there are also important physical differences between the two continents.

North America has a great central plains area, stretching from the Appalachians to the Rockies, drained by the Mississippi River system into the Gulf of Mexico.

South America has not one, but three, great lowland areas. They are separated from each other by highlands, and the rivers which drain them empty into the sea in widely separated places.

Another difference is that South America has no broad coastal plain like the one which stretches down the east coast of North America from Maine to Florida.

These facts are important in the history of the two continents. The coastal plain of North America afforded an easy entrance to European settlers, while the coastal highlands of South America made it difficult to penetrate inland except up the rivers.

The great central plains of the United States were easy for settlers to occupy and cultivate. It was easy to build roads and railroads across this great open area, and the communications network helped to tie the United States together. It also spurred the growth of trade and industry.

South America's mountain barriers between the lowlands made communication very difficult. The lowlands did not serve to tie the continent together. They are still relatively undeveloped. Difficult communications have kept South America split up.

The plant life of South America is divided into several broad zones corresponding to the climate and landforms. In the hot, rainy areas of the north is the tropical rainforest. The trees of the rainforest are

There are few islands along the coast of South America, except in the far southwest. The largest are the Tierra del Fuego, off the southern tip of the continent, Marajó, in the mouth of the Amazon, and Chiloé, in southern Chile.

The most important islands are Trinidad, off the northern coast, which produces asphalt and oil, and the Falkland Islands in the south Atlantic, an important whaling base. Both these are British possessions.

Leo Matiz—Pix

The plain of the Orinoco River is vast and flat, always too wet or too dry for growing crops.

Some passes in Bolivia's towering mountains are higher than the peaks of the Rocky Mountains—13,000 feet.

tall and straight. They are always green. They grow so close that their tops interlace and form a dense canopy.

There is too little light on the forest floor to let undergrowth grow, but along the streams, where the light gets through, the undergrowth is so thick that a man can hardly penetrate it.

North and south of the equatorial rainforest lie regions where the weather is hot, but the rainfall is not evenly distributed throughout the year. The plants must be able to survive a dry season.

The predominant vegetation here is the savanna, a grassland with scattered, small trees and shrubs, or, where the land is moister, open woodlands. The grass may grow up to 12 feet tall. Along the streams grow taller trees. In the dry season, many of the trees and shrubs lose their leaves, and the grass becomes dry and brown.

The Andes form a very complex zone. In the north the plant life is like that of the nearby lowlands — rainforest in wet areas and grass or scrub in dry areas.

Further south, where it is cooler and drier, needle-leaved trees and deciduous (leaf-shedding) trees replace the broadleaved evergreens of the rainforest.

Above the tree line the slopes and plateaus are covered with short grass and shrubs. The vegetation becomes sparser as it approaches the snow line. Above the snow line there is no plant life at all.

South of the Brazilian Highlands the continent becomes drier. The land is covered with grass, much like the prairies of North America. In the cold, dry region of Patagonia, deserts replace grasslands.

The cool, rainy southwest coast region is covered with a dense forest of mixed needle-leaved and deciduous trees.

Hugh A. Wilmar

Two white-faced monkeys study an iguana, the largest lizard of the American tropics.

Harold Schultz—Birnback

The tapir's family goes back to prehistoric times. This is the small, shy kind of the lowlands.

Giant anteaters tear down termite nests with long claws and sweep up insects with sticky tongues.

James R. Simon

SOUTH AMERICAN ANIMALS

Because South America is isolated from the other land masses of the world, except for the narrow land bridge of the Isthmus of Panama, its animal life is quite different from that of other continents.

Some familiar species of the "Old World" are entirely lacking. Others have developed in a different direction from their Old World relatives. And some of South America's animals are found only in the western hemisphere.

An interesting fact is that none of South America's animals reaches a very great size. The largest land animal is the tapir, a piglike creature with a short, flexible trunk. The tapir reaches a length of 6 to 8 feet and stands about 3 feet tall.

Another South American mammal is the manatee, or sea cow. The manatee, which lives entirely in the water, is shaped like a seal, but its face resembles a calf's. It sometimes makes a noise like the mooing of a cow. The manatee, which lives on water plants, grows to a length of nine to fifteen feet. When full-grown, it may weigh over a ton. Its skin is black and nearly hairless.

The greatest variety of animal life is found in the warm, wet rainforests of the Amazon Valley and the higher lands bordering it. Near the streams live tapirs and

The three-foot capybara of the Amazon jungle is the largest rodent in the world.

Hugh A. Wilmar

Russ Kinne—Photo Researchers

Hugh A. Wilmar

Coatis are members of the raccoon family. They have long snouts for poking into burrows.

This baby sloth looks lively, but when grown it will hang lazily in trees most of the day.

These jaguars are the same kind. Occasionally a black jaguar is born to a spotted mother.

Hugh A. Wilmar

three-foot capybaras, the world's largest rodents. There are giant anteaters and armadillos. There are vicious jaguars and other members of the cat family. There are twenty-foot boa constrictors and many poi-

James R. Simon

The green boa lives in trees. It is not poisonous, but crushes its prey by coiling around it.

The parrots of the jungles are brilliant and noisy. Their flashing colors are everywhere.

James R. Simon

sonous snakes such as the deadly fer-de-lance and bushmaster.

Chattering monkeys swarm through the trees in the daytime. The noise of the frogs and toads is deafening at night. Ants and termites are everywhere. Beetles grow to giant size — as much as six inches long. There are fireflies with red, yellow, and blue lights. One spider grows large enough to hunt birds.

The peccary, a wild pig, runs in bands of a hundred or more in the Amazon region. They have occasionally attacked small cities. The familiar raccoon also lives there, with its cousins the coatis and the kinkajous. The sloth, the slowest animal in the world, spends its life hanging upside down from tree branches. Rodents run on the forest floor, and millions of bats fly among the trees. Among them is the vampire bat, which lives on blood which it sucks from animals and human beings. It is greatly feared as a carrier of rabies.

Manatees and fresh-water dolphins live in the lakes and streams. The rivers abound with fish: some large like the giant catfish, some dangerous like the electric eel and the piranha. The bloodthirsty schools of piranha can strip the flesh from a person or animal in minutes. Other water-dwellers include turtles, lizards, and caymans (a kind of crocodile).

Many of the birds are brilliantly colored —parrots, macaws, toucans, and great flocks of parakeets. Birds of prey soar above the trees. And there are flocks of waterfowl on the lakes and streams.

On the open plains of Argentina live other sorts of animals: foxes, hares, armadillos, and deer. The rhea, a relative of the ostrich, lives here. In the rivers are salmon, trout, and other food fish.

Animals are relatively few in the highlands of the Andes. The llamas and their relatives, the guanacos and alpacas, graze on the scanty grasses. They are small, humpless relatives of the camel. Rodents like the guinea pig and the chinchilla are

Russ Kinne—Photo Researchers

Burden-carrying llamas also supply wool and meat.

James R. Simon

Graceful flamingoes wade in a quiet stream.

common. The condor, a giant vulture with an 8- to 11-foot wingspread, soars in lonely places.

The gulls, terns, and other sea birds that nest on the islands off the coast of Peru are unusually numerous. Scientists once made a count. They found that, on just one small part of one island, there were about five and a half million birds. This number would eat a thousand tons of fish a day! Their dried excrement, or guano, is a valuable fertilizer. The Peruvian government now protects the birds in order to ensure a future supply of guano.

James R. Simon

Above: Armadillos are protected by bony scales.
Below: Amazon crocodiles rarely molest people.

Piranhas—"cannibal fish"—have razor-like teeth. A school of them can clean a carcass in minutes.

Courtesy of the Johnson Motor Co.

Hugh A. Wilmar

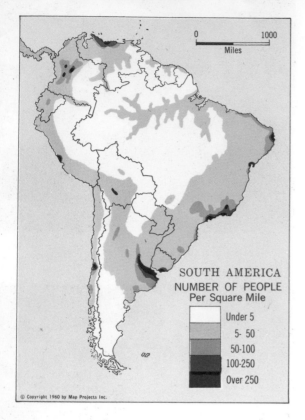

SOUTH AMERICA
NUMBER OF PEOPLE
Per Square Mile

	Under 5
	5- 50
	50-100
	100-250
	Over 250

© Copyright 1960 by Map Projects Inc.

This little Colombian girl, dressed in her Sunday best, is on her way home from church.

Charles Perry Weimer—House of Photography

PEOPLE OF SOUTH AMERICA

In the United States, there is no such complete mixture of races as there is in South America. There, more than half the population is one combination or another of white, Indian, and Negro.

Indians lived all over the continent when the first white explorers arrived. About three quarters of them were in the northern Andes, near the west coast. There, farming was much easier than in the tropical lowlands, where the soils were generally poor and the many insect pests took their toll of the crops.

Two very advanced civilizations lived in the mountain highlands. The largest was the Inca Empire, which included the Quechuas and Aymaras of Ecuador, Bolivia, and Peru and a few Araucanians in northern Chile. A smaller group was the Chibchas of Colombia.

Other South American tribes were backward by comparison. Most Araucanians lived in central and southern Chile. The Tupi and Guaraní were the tribes of Brazil and Paraguay. The Caribs and Arawaks were scattered all over the north. They all lived in small, separate groups, hunting and fishing and doing a little farming.

On the Argentine plains were the Puelche and Abipones, warlike hunters living mainly on the flesh of the rhea, an ostrich-like bird, and the guanaco.

The first white explorers were men from southern Spain and Portugal, where there was little prejudice against marrying people of different races. Many of them married Indian women. Their children were called *mestizo* (mixed-blood).

Today, by far the largest racial strain in South America is Indian or part Indian. In Colombia, Venezuela, and Chile, two thirds of the people are mestizos. In Paraguay, almost the entire population is mestizo.

An Arawak Indian mother travels with her three children in a flat-bottomed wooden canoe.

This young boy is one of the many Negro people who work on coffee plantations in Brazil.

The Latacunga market in Ecuador is in an ancient Inca town, once destroyed by an earthquake.

There is no country where there are not some mestizos.

Some Indians did not mix with whites. In Ecuador, Peru, and Bolivia, more than half the people are pure Indian. They live almost entirely in the mountains.

When the Portuguese started settling the east coast of Brazil, they found only a few Indians. These Indians were not willing to work on plantations, so the Portuguese brought Negro slaves from Africa. Today, Brazil has more than five million Negro and part-Negro citizens. Most of them live on the east coast and in the central western part of Brazil near the gold fields. Along the rest of Brazil's coast and along some of the rivers in the interior, the people are mixed Portuguese, Indian, and Negro.

Another group of Negroes lives on the northeast coast of Colombia. These people, too, are the descendants of slaves from Africa.

There were no settlements on the land south of the Río de la Plata until the nineteenth century. When European settlers did come, the Indians had been driven out. As a result, Argentina's people are almost entirely white. The number of Negroes is small and there are only a few *mestizo* gauchos, the wandering horsemen of the pampas.

Strangely, in this great mixture of people, there are a few groups whose way of living has changed very little as to time or place. In the Guiana jungles there are villages of "bush Negroes," the descendants of runaway slaves. They live as their ancestors did in Africa in the seventeenth century. In British Guiana is a large settlement of Asian Indians, complete with Hindu temples and typical Asian customs.

There are also colonies of European immigrants who have clung to the customs of the "old country."

Many businessmen live and work in São Paulo, the commercial and financial center of Brazil.

Rex—Birnback

The beaded hat and coin-spangled belt are special fiesta decorations of the Araucanians of Chile.

Wolfe Worldwide Films, Los Angeles 24, Calif.

The adventurous, hard-riding, hard-fighting cowboys of South America are called *gauchos*.

Fujihira—Monkmeyer

A Quechua of Ecuador plays a wooden flute. Most of the Inca peoples were Quechuas.

There are Indians at the southern tip of the continent who live as their ancestors did in the Stone Age. Others, in the Andes, have not changed their ways since the days of the Inca Empire. The forests of the Amazon Valley are thinly populated by Caribs and Arawaks, still living much as they did four centuries ago.

There is very little racial prejudice in South America. But there is a tremendous difference in the way the rich and the poor live. The rich live in beautiful houses and have many servants.

But most of the people are poor. Those on farms and around mines live in wooden shacks or mud houses. They rarely get enough to eat. They have little money for clothes.

Only about one third of South America's people live in cities, compared to two thirds in the United States. City people live much as North American city people do. But more of them live in slums and there are fewer comfortable middle-class houses.

This young Aymara boy wears the typical hat and cape of Bolivians of the Lake Titicaca region.

Ewing Krainin—Photo Researchers

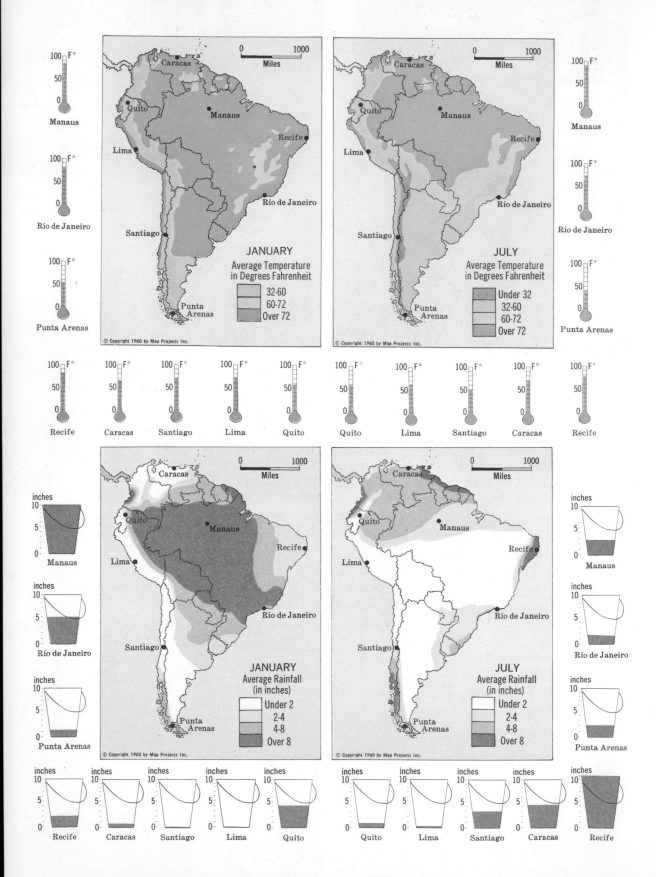

Manaus

Rio de Janeiro

Punta Arenas

JANUARY
Average Temperature
in Degrees Fahrenheit
- 32-60
- 60-72
- Over 72

© Copyright 1960 by Map Projects Inc.

Caracas

Quito

Manaus

Lima

Recife

Rio de Janeiro

Santiago

Punta Arenas

JULY
Average Temperature
in Degrees Fahrenheit
- Under 32
- 32-60
- 60-72
- Over 72

© Copyright 1960 by Map Projects Inc.

Manaus

Rio de Janeiro

Punta Arenas

Recife   Caracas   Santiago   Lima   Quito

Quito   Lima   Santiago   Caracas   Recife

JANUARY
Average Rainfall
(in inches)
- Under 2
- 2-4
- 4-8
- Over 8

© Copyright 1960 by Map Projects Inc.

JULY
Average Rainfall
(in inches)
- Under 2
- 2-4
- 4-8
- Over 8

© Copyright 1960 by Map Projects Inc.

Manaus

Rio de Janeiro

Punta Arenas

Manaus

Rio de Janeiro

Punta Arenas

Recife   Caracas   Santiago   Lima   Quito

Quito   Lima   Santiago   Caracas   Recife

CLIMATE

Most of South America lies south of the equator. South of the equator, the seasons are reversed from those north of the equator. When it is summer in New York, Chicago, or St. Louis, it is winter in Buenos Aires and Rio de Janeiro. South of the equator, July is the coldest month and January is the warmest. Christmas comes just after midsummer.

In the United States the farther south one goes the warmer the weather becomes. This is because we are getting closer to the equator. But the farther south one goes in South America, after crossing the equator, the colder the weather becomes.

The northern part of South America lies across the equator. But at its southern tip it is nearer to the South Pole than any other continent in the world except Antarctica itself. Cape Horn is as far from the equator as Hudson Bay, in Canada.

The southern part of the continent would be as cold as Canada except for the oceans on each side of it. Since the land is narrow here, the oceans have a strong influence on the climate. Winter temperatures seldom go much below freezing, except in the mountains. Summer temperatures average between 50 and 60 degrees.

Where the land is broader, temperatures are not as much controlled by the oceans. These regions are more like the places in North America which are the same distance from the equator.

Much of South America lies within the tropics, the zone on each side of the equator in which the sun's rays strike the earth directly at least one day each year. Because the tropics receive so much sunlight, the climate is generally warm all year round.

We often think of a tropical climate as being always hot and damp. But this is not necessarily so. While there are regions in the Guianas and the Amazon valley that are hot and damp, there are also dry, hot regions in the northeast of Brazil and the northern coast of Venezuela. The west coast in Peru and northern Chile is a cool cloudy desert, because of the influence of a cold ocean current along the shore.

As we know, the climate of any region becomes cooler as the land rises. The upper slopes and high plateaus of the northern Andes are cool, although they lie within the tropics. The higher mountains are snow-capped all year.

The city of Quito, Ecuador, which lies almost directly on the equator at a height of 9,350 feet above sea level, has an average annual temperature of 54 degrees. The difference between the warmest and the coldest months is less than one degree.

Throughout most of the Andes there is greater difference between day and night temperatures than between summer and winter temperatures.

Although many people think that the equator is the hottest region on earth, this is not true. The lowlands of the Amazon basin are hot and steamy, but they are not as hot as Kansas in the corn-growing season. And the higher lands near the equator are relatively cool. The hottest place in South America is the Chaco region of northern Argentina.

Southern Argentina is cool and dry. The weather changes constantly and there are many blustery storms, but they bring little rain. Southern Chile is cool and stormy and very wet. Middle Chile has mild, rainy winters and warm, dry summers, much like southern California.

Most of northern South America has rain every month of the year. In many places the rainfall averages over 80 inches a year. By comparison, the northeastern United States averages about 40 inches a year. Farther south the rainfall becomes less.

Climate is important to South Americans because the amount of rainfall and warmth determines what crops they can grow and where they can grow them.

USE OF THE LAND

Man's use of the land is determined by such things as the nature of the soil, the amount of rainfall and when it falls, the temperature, and the natural resources available. It is also determined in part by man himself.

Farming and stock-raising are the chief activities of South America. Farming is found wherever the soil is fertile enough to grow crops and there is enough water (either from rainfall or irrigation) available. Large herds of livestock are raised on the natural grasslands which occupy so much of the continent.

The forests yield many valuable products, but they are generally gathered from wild plants, not cultivated. Minerals are found in the highlands, and there is oil in the lowlands.

There are great areas, however, which are useless for farming because the climate is too cold, because of insect pests, because of flooding, or because the water supply is too irregular.

The area in the north covered by the tropical rainforest is one example. Although the constant rain and warmth encourage a lush growth of wild plants, they have also washed the plant nutrients out of the soil. The soil is too poor to support crops for long. There are many insect pests. And the river valleys are flooded for part of the year.

Because South America has such great contrasts of altitude, crops in many areas must be grown according to elevation. In the hot lowlands and in the hot, low valleys and on the lower slopes of the mountains grow crops such as sugar, cotton, and cacao, which need constant warmth. Grains can be raised at altitudes up to about 10,000 or 12,000 feet. Coffee is grown on the middle slopes. Potatoes, which originated on the high, bleak Andean plateaus, can be grown even higher than the grains.

Above the upper limits of potato cultivation, the grasslands are used for pasturing hardy llamas and sheep. Sheep are also

Small settlements of tenant farmers grow crops on fertile hillsides near the Magdalena River.

raised in Patagonia, where the land is too poor and the climate too cold for anything else to be raised commercially.

The lowlands of northeastern Argentina and Uruguay, with their moderate climate, are the principal producer of grain and livestock. The level land and fertile soil favor large-scale farming. Much grain is also grown in central Chile, where the climate is like that of California.

In the United States about one sixth of the people are farmers, but they produce enough food to feed twenty times their number. In South America nearly two thirds of the people are farmers, but most of them grow only enough food for themselves.

One reason that the farmers grow so little food is that many of them live in isolated mountain valleys or back-country settlements. They have no way to get their products to market, and so have no reason to raise more than will satisfy their immediate needs.

Another reason is that much of the farm land belongs to big landowners. The landowners use the best land for commercial crops like sugar, coffee, and cotton, which they sell on world markets. Or they may use the best land for raising cattle, horses, or sheep, and for crops to feed the animals.

The poor land is turned over to the tenant farmers for their own use. They raise such foods as corn, rice, and beans. Yields are low because of the poverty of the soil. In most South American countries, corn takes up more space than all other crops combined.

The great rainforest of the Amazon basin yields many valuable products. Some of them are tropical woods, fibers, wax, vegetable oils, and nuts. But the plants of any one kind are widely scattered instead of growing in stands. This makes collecting them difficult and expensive.

The scrub forests of the Chaco region in northern Argentina and Paraguay and the pine forests of southern Brazil are also

George Hunter—Annan Photo Features
Goats can be raised in the high mountains where the land is too barren for crops.

Charles Perry Weimer—House of Photography
Some farmers of the Andes use modern machinery, but most farming is still very primitive.

These Peruvian sugar growers still work with the ancient foot plow to plant their crops.
Wolfe Worldwide Films, Los Angeles 24, Calif.

Rosene—Shostal

Wheat is harvested in December in central Chile. Machinery is used, but older methods are common.

Courtesy of the Pan American Coffee Bureau

Coffee is a tremendous industry in Brazil. Brazil is the world's largest coffee producer.

exploited. The dense forests of the southwestern coast are not utilized, as they are too far from population centers.

South America has some of the world's greatest mineral deposits. Most of them are found in the highland or mountain areas, where volcanic activity and the folding and cracking of the earth's crust have brought them close to the surface.

Brazil has what is possibly the world's largest and richest iron ore reserve. Chile has rich copper mines and the only natural nitrate deposits in the world. Venezuela has iron ore and one of the world's greatest oil fields. British and Dutch Guiana produce over a third of the world's supply of bauxite (aluminum ore).

Some of the many other minerals are: tin, tungsten, manganese, vanadium, lead, zinc, mercury, platinum, and iodine.

Much of this mineral wealth has not been exploited because of the difficulty of transporting it to market and because labor has been hard to get. And fuel for refining the ores is scarce in South America.

Despite these handicaps, the Spaniards operated gold and silver mines in the bleak Andes, because these metals were so valuable that it was profitable.

Today the need of North American and European industry for raw materials has made it profitable to exploit the less glamorous resources of iron, copper, and the other basic metals.

This copper mine has just been opened. It is in the Atacama Desert and is completely modern.

Courtesy of ANACONDA

EXPLORATION AND SETTLEMENT

Scientists believe that the first people to come to South America were from Asia. They may have come from Siberia over the Bering Strait to Alaska and gradually spread over North and South America.

Thousands of years later Christopher Columbus called them Indians because when he landed on the Bahama Islands he thought he had reached India.

Columbus and other explorers sailed up and down the northeast coast of South America for twenty years looking for a short route to India. They did not explore far inland, but they claimed large parts of the continent for Spain and Portugal.

When Ferdinand Magellan finally found the passage that the earlier explorers had been seeking at the tip of South America, the search for the route to India stopped. The conquest of South America began.

The Spaniards landed first on the north coast and worked their way far into the interior. They conquered the Indian people of Peru, Chile, Ecuador, and Colombia. They crossed the Andes, and one explorer sailed to the mouth of the Amazon. They established colonies in the region of the Río de la Plata and later in Paraguay.

While the Spaniards were exploring the continent from the west, the Portuguese were working westward from the east. Within a short time they had occupied all of Brazil. Spain and Portugal now had a firm hold on the continent.

The South American explorers were not especially interested in new places to live. The Spaniards were said to have come because of "greed, gold, and God." Many of them had a burning desire to convert the Indians to Christianity. There was real need for gold in Spain where a long war had impoverished the country. And many Spaniards who had never had wealth or land were extremely greedy.

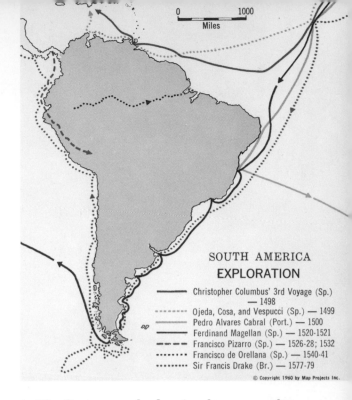

SOUTH AMERICA
EXPLORATION

———— Christopher Columbus' 3rd Voyage (Sp.) — 1498
············ Ojeda, Cosa, and Vespucci (Sp.) — 1499
———— Pedro Alvares Cabral (Port.) — 1500
———— Ferdinand Magellan (Sp.) — 1520-1521
– – – Francisco Pizarro (Sp.) — 1526-28; 1532
·········· Francisco de Orellana (Sp.) — 1540-41
·········· Sir Francis Drake (Br.) — 1577-79

© Copyright 1960 by Map Projects Inc.

The Portuguese had a simpler reason for coming. They only wanted to get rich. Finding no gold, they brought Negro slaves and grew sugar cane to sell in Europe. It was so profitable that most of the countries in Europe tried to start plantations on the mainland of South America or on the Caribbean islands. But, except in the Guianas, they were pushed out by Spain and Portugal.

The continent was divided into four large areas called viceroyalties. (Viceroyalties are territories governed by a viceroy—a representative of the king or queen.) Three of them were Spanish—the Viceroyalties of New Granada, Peru, and La Plata. One was Portuguese — the Viceroyalty of Brazil. They included all of the continent except the far south, where there were no settlers, and the Guianas.

The American and French revolutions at the end of the eighteenth century brought a strong desire for freedom to the colonists. They fought wars of independence and freed themselves. The Spanish viceroyalties split up into separate countries. After several wars between the new countries, the map of South America looked much as it does today.

VENEZUELA

COLOMBIA

BR. GUIANA

DUTCH GUIANA

FR. GUIANA

Tobago
Trinidad

0   1000
Miles
© Copyright 1960 by Map Projects Inc.

ECUADOR

Equator

Cape São Roque

PERU

B R A Z I L

—10°

BOLIVIA

—20°

PARAGUAY

Tropic of Capricorn

30°

• PACIFIC

ATLANTIC OCEAN

—30°

CHILE

URUGUAY

OCEAN

ARGENTINA

90°
—40°

—50°

Strait of Magellan

(Br.)
FALKLAND
ISLANDS

100°

TIERRA
DEL
FUEGO   Cape Horn

TRANSPORTATION

South America depends heavily on the ocean for transportation. Roads and railroads lead from the interior to the seaports. Very few of them lead from one city to another.

The main links between population centers are ships. Airplanes are being used more and more in South America. They are very efficient for passengers and mail, but they cannot carry bulky or very heavy freight cheaply.

In the mountain countries, railroads are so expensive to build that freight costs are very high. In Venezuela a two-hundred-mile railroad had to have 217 bridges and 86 tunnels. As a result, many goods are still shipped by oxcart and mule.

Recently more all-weather roads have been built. Trucks can carry goods for one twentieth the cost of mules where there are roads. But there are still very few roads, particularly from the west coast to the east.

SOUTH AMERICA

——— MAIN
RAILROADS

0   1000
Miles

© Copyright 1960 by Map Projects Inc.

SOUTH AMERICA

——— MAIN AIR
ROUTES

0   1000
Miles

© Copyright 1960 by Map Projects Inc.

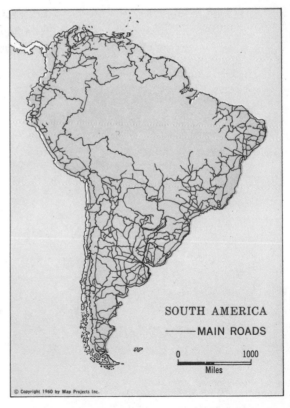

SOUTH AMERICA

——— MAIN ROADS

0   1000
Miles

© Copyright 1960 by Map Projects Inc.

In the whole enormous length of Chile—2,740 miles—there are only half-a-dozen routes over the mountains.

Plains countries like Argentina and Uruguay have miles of railroads. On flat land they cost very little to build. Argentina has railroads criss-crossed all over the pampas. But it has few all-weather roads because the dusty, rockless soil blows away in the dry season and turns to a sea of mud when it rains. Uruguay has plenty of gravel for road building, so it has as many roads as railroads.

The north and northeast depend on rivers for transportation. The Guianas have almost no all-weather roads or railroads. Most products are loaded directly onto ocean-going ships which go up the rivers, but they cannot go far because the rivers are interrupted by falls. One river is so narrow that ships must be towed backwards to the loading point because they cannot turn when they reach it.

Brazil's system of roads and railroads is entirely on or near the east and northeast coasts. All other transportation is handled by the rivers. The Amazon can take ships right up to the foothills of the Andes.

MAJOR CITIES OF SOUTH AMERICA

South America's cities are not as old as some in Asia and Europe, but many of them are older than the leading cities of North America. Some of them, like Quito, Bogotá, and Cuzco were capitals of the Indian civilizations of the highlands. Others were founded in the sixteenth and seventeenth centuries by the Spanish and Portuguese conquistadors as ports and administrative centers. Lima, Buenos Aires, and Rio de Janeiro are examples of this type of city. Few developed as trading centers, for there was little trade between the regions of South America.

In the warmer regions of South America, the leading cities are located in the highlands, where the climate is comfortable for people of European origin. The cities were generally built in valleys, where food for the inhabitants could be raised, or along navigable rivers. Even today the largest cities are those which can be reached by boat.

Some were built as centers for the mining regions which produced so much of Spain's wealth in the sixteenth and seventeenth centuries. Some developed as residential towns for the wealthy landowners.

Because industry came late to South America, manufacturing has tended to concentrate in already established population centers, where workers can easily be obtained. Few new industrial towns have been founded.

Although many of South America's cities have picturesque old buildings, today they are better known for their modern architecture and broad, beautiful avenues. Carácas, Venezuela, is one of the most modern cities in the world.

South America's cities have been growing rapidly in recent years with the development of industry and better communications. People from the villages and farms flock to the cities to escape the monotony and poverty of rural life.

Buenos Aires, the capital and chief seaport of Argentina, looks much like Paris.

Courtesy of Pan American World Airways

The cone-shaped peak of Sugar Loaf Mountain guards the entrance to Rio de Janeiro's harbor.

Here are brief descriptions of some of the largest cities of South America.

BUENOS AIRES, the capital of Argentina, was founded in 1536. Soon abandoned because of Indian attacks, it was reoccupied in 1581. In 1880 it was made into a federal district like Washington, D.C.

Buenos Aires is a leading port and industrial city, as well as the outlet of the rich grain and stock-raising districts of the pampas. About one fifth of the population of Argentina lives in or near Buenos Aires.

SÃO PAULO is the largest and fastest-growing city of Brazil. It is the capital of Brazil's richest agricultural state and the center of the coffee district. It has a large and diversified industry.

São Paulo, built on the Brazilian Highlands just behind the coast, is served by the port of Santos. São Paulo remained a frontier town until the coffee boom of the late nineteenth century.

RIO DE JANEIRO, the capital of Brazil, is built on a deep, landlocked bay. It was founded in 1567 by the Portuguese and has served as capital since 1763. In 1960 it is planned to move the capital to the new city of Brasilia, in the center of the country.

Rio is primarily a shipping center, though it has some industry. Its beautiful setting and attractive beaches also make it a popular tourist resort. Rio de Janeiro is well known for its modern buildings.

São Paulo is a thriving manufacturing city, the fastest growing and largest city in Brazil.

Joe Barnell—Shostal

Montevideo, Uruguay, is so pleasant that tourists come to it from Brazil and Argentina.

RECIFE, Brazil's third largest city, is named after a coral reef which shelters its harbor. It is a shipping center for sugar, cotton, tobacco, castor oil, and hides. It was founded in 1530 by the Portuguese.

MONTEVIDEO, the capital of Uruguay, is the center of a prosperous agricultural region and a leading seaport. About one third of the country's people live there. Founded in 1726, the city was much fought over by the Spanish and Portuguese. Montevideo, with its pleasant climate and inviting beaches, is a favorite resort for wealthy Argentinians and Brazilians.

LA PAZ, the highest large city in the world, lies in the Andes, almost 12,000 feet

Quito, Ecuador, one of the highest cities in the world, looks like a colonial Spanish town.

Ewing Krainin—Alpha

The Spanish founded La Paz in a deep canyon sunk in a windswept plateau. It is 12,000 feet high.

Ewing Krainin—Alpha

Joe Barnell—Shostal

Most of the old buildings in Santiago, Chile, have been destroyed by earthquakes. It now is a modern city.

above sea level. The city is built in the bottom of a deep canyon to provide some shelter from the cold winds of the bleak plateau or *Altiplano*. Despite its inconvenient location, La Paz is the industrial center of Bolivia. The city was founded in 1548 by the Spaniards.

QUITO, the capital of Ecuador, is another highland city. It is built on the slope of a dead volcano. The average daily temperature never changes by more than three tenths of a degree. Quito was once one of the capitals of the Inca empire. The city has over fifty churches.

SANTIAGO, the capital of Chile, is situated on a broad plain at the foot of the

Lima is the capital and cultural center of Peru. The cathedral on the Plaza de Armas dates back to the sixteenth century. Lima's San Marcos University, founded in 1551, is one of the oldest in the Americas.

Courtesy of PANAGRA

Bogotá, Colombia, is built so high in the Andes that it is most easily reached by airplane.

Courtesy of the Grace Line

LIMA, the capital of Peru, was founded by Pizarro, the Spanish conquistador, in 1535. For over 300 years it was the largest and wealthiest city of South America. It still dominates the life of the country. The University of San Marcos (founded 1551) is the oldest in South America.

BOGOTÁ, the capital of Colombia, is a famous cultural center. Built on the site of an Indian capital, Bogotá was founded by the Spaniards in 1538. There are several universities, the oldest founded in 1572, and students come from many lands. Many artists and writers also live in Bogotá. There is little industry.

CARACAS, the capital of Venezuela, is located six miles inland from the coast in the mountains. Three thousand feet above sea level, it has a comfortable climate. Founded in 1567, the city has been largely rebuilt in recent years and is famous for its modern architecture. The center of a fertile farming region, Caracas also has growing industries.

Andes. It has a pleasant climate. It is the commercial and industrial center of the country. About every seventh Chilean lives in or near Santiago.

Founded in 1541, it has been destroyed by Indian attacks, earthquakes, and floods, but has grown steadily to be South America's fourth largest city.

Much of Caracas has been completely rebuilt recently. Oil has paid for the modern roads and buildings.

Hamilton Wright Organization, Inc.

A notorious prison colony once occupied Devil's Island off the coast of French Guiana.

NORTHERN SOUTH AMERICA

Five countries extend along South America's northern coast. Two of them—Colombia and Venezuela—are independent. The other three—British, French, and Dutch Guiana (the last also called Surinam)—are European colonies. The total area of these countries is nearly one million square miles.

Each of the countries of northern South America has a relatively narrow strip of coastal lowland. Inland are rugged highlands with deep gorges cut by streams. Venezuela and Colombia also have interior lowlands in the river valleys and a number of intermountain basins.

Each country is sharply divided into regions by the natural barriers of the highlands, so that the people of each region have had, until the development of modern transportation, very little contact with each other.

These countries lie across what is called the "heat equator," the belt of highest temperatures. The whole region is sharply divided into lowlands and mountains. Some of the lowlands are hot and steamy, with no relief at any season. Others are dry and hot. Even some of the highlands are hot, because they are not quite high enough to be cooled by the upper air.

Most of the coast is low, but there are a few places where the highlands come within a few miles of the ocean. The coast of the Guianas is formed of silt from the Amazon River. The river carries enormous quantities of silt out to sea, and the ocean current sweeps it northwest along the coast and deposits it along the shore of the Guianas, where it forms long sandbars.

Back of these silt deposits are marshy areas, flooded at high tide by the ocean and crossed by rivers on their way to the Caribbean Sea. In some places this coast is fifty miles wide, but much of it is only fifteen miles wide.

This low coastal strip continues into Venezuela past the mouth of the Orinoco River until it is interrupted by the Venezuelan Highlands, a branch of the Andes. This highland rises at the edge of the sea. The coastal strip then continues around Lake Maracaibo as a hot, flat plain into Colombia.

In Colombia the coastal lowland is again interrupted by a high group of mountains west of Lake Maracaibo. From these mountains around the northern tip of the continent, past the border of Panama, and on down the west coast, the coastal land is low and hot.

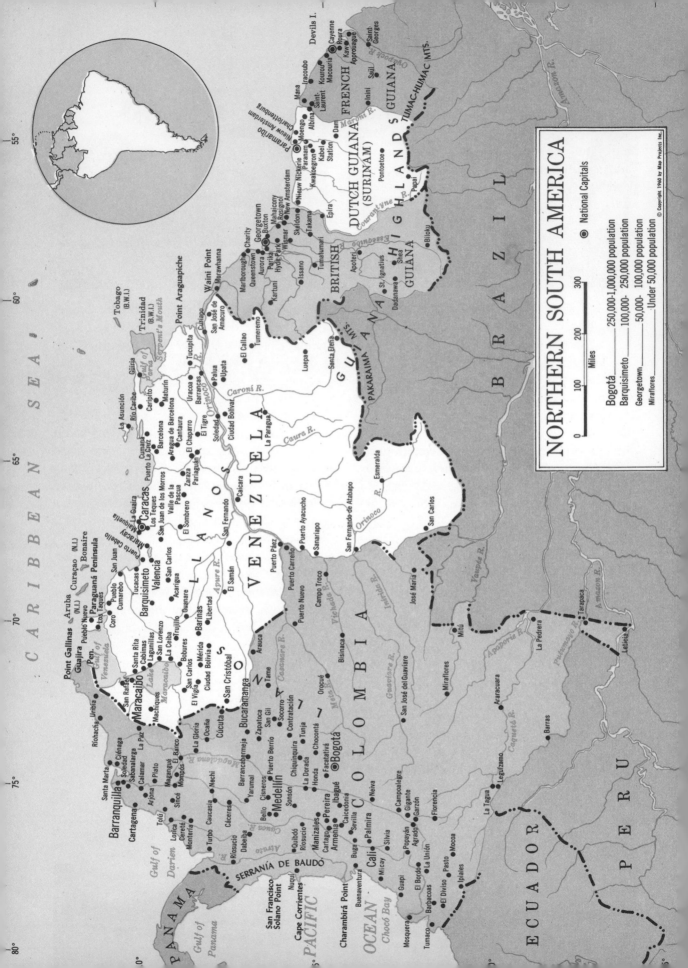

NORTHERN SOUTH AMERICA

◉ National Capitals

Miles			
0	100	200	300

Bogotá — 250,000–1,000,000 population
Barquisimeto — 100,000– 250,000 population
Georgetown — 50,000– 100,000 population
Miraflores — Under 50,000 population

© Copyright 1960 by Map Projects Inc.

CARIBBEAN SEA

PACIFIC OCEAN

PANAMA

COLOMBIA

VENEZUELA

BRAZIL

ECUADOR

PERU

BRITISH GUIANA

DUTCH GUIANA (SURINAM)

FRENCH GUIANA

GUIANA HIGHLANDS

LLANOS

SONSON

GUIANA MTS.

PAKARAIMA MTS.

TUMACHUMAC MTS.

SERRANÍA DE BAUDÓ

Gulf of Darien

Gulf of Panama

Choco Bay

Gulf of Venezuela

Lake Maracaibo

Gulf of Paria

Serpent's Mouth

Orinoco R.

Amazon R.

Caroni R.

Caura R.

Apure R.

Meta R.

Casanare R.

Guaviare R.

Vichada R.

Inirida R.

Vaupés R.

Caquetá R.

Putumayo R.

Apaporis R.

Magdalena R.

Cauca R.

Atrato R.

Sinu R.

Oyapock R.

Maroni R.

Courantyne R.

Essequibo R.

Trinidad (B.W.I.)

Tobago (B.W.I.)

Aruba (N.I.)

Curaçao (N.I.)

Bonaire (N.I.)

Devils I.

Paraguaná Peninsula

Guajira Pen.

Point Gallinas

Point Araguapiche

Waini Point

Cape Corrientes

San Francisco Solano Point

Charambirá Point

Cities and towns

Caracas, Maracaibo, Barquisimeto, Valencia, Bogotá, Medellín, Cali, Barranquilla, Cartagena, Georgetown, Paramaribo, Cayenne, Bucaramanga, Cúcuta, San Cristóbal, Mérida, Maracay, Los Teques, La Guaira, Maiquetía, Puerto Cabello, Coro, Coro, Barcelona, Cumaná, Maturín, Ciudad Bolívar, Santa Marta, Riohacha, Valledupar, Montería, Sincelejo, Manizales, Pereira, Armenia, Ibagué, Neiva, Pasto, Popayán, Tunja, Sogamoso, Villavicencio

The principal highlands of Northern South America are the Guiana Highlands in the east and the Andes in the west. The Guiana Highlands are densely forested and very rugged. This almost unexplored area makes up most of the land of the Guianas and about half the land of Venezuela.

The rivers which come down from its hills and plateaus are interrupted by many falls. One of them, Kaieteur Falls in British Guiana, is one of the highest in the world. It drops straight down, 741 feet!

The Andes in northern South America divide and spread like three huge fingers into separate chains. Many of the peaks are so high they are always covered with snow. The slopes are covered with dense forest.

The western and middle chains are within Colombia. The eastern chain also extends into Venezuela.

Between the western and middle chains is the hot lowland floodplain of the Cauca River, which flows toward the north coast. Dividing the middle from the eastern chain is the valley of the Magdalena River.

Between the eastern chain of the Andes and the Guiana Highlands lies the vast, empty plain of the Orinoco River. It is called the Orinoco Llanos ("*llanos*" means "plains"). About 600 miles long and 200 miles wide, these nearly flat plains slope gradually from the Andes foothills to the broad river which drains them.

Charles Perry Weimer—House of Photography

Herders must slosh through shallow water to round up their cattle near the Orinoco River.

During the five-month rainy season, the wandering streams that cross the llanos cannot carry off the water, and most of the plain is flooded. During the dry season, the trees and shrubs lose their leaves, the grasses dry up, and the smaller streams have no water at all.

Few people live in the Orinoco Llanos. The region is used for grazing cattle, which are driven from place to place to escape the floodwaters and to find fresh pasture.

Most of the twenty million people of northern South America live on or near the coasts. About nine tenths of the land is almost unoccupied.

About two thirds of the people of Colombia and Venezuela are mestizos and one fifth are white. The rest are Negroes and a few pure Indians. In the Guianas, less than three people in a hundred are white.

The city of Medellín, in a high mountain valley, is the chief market and manufacturing city of Colombia.

Charles Perry Weimer—House of Photography

Fritz Henle—Photo Researchers

This Hindu farmer in Surinam threshes his rice by letting cattle trample the grain from the chaff.

Fujihira—Monkmeyer

Buxton Village in British Guiana is a typical Asian Indian village. These women are Hindus.

The Guianas

The Guianas are a heavily forested region. The early Spanish and Portuguese conquerors, who disliked forests, made no serious attempts to settle there. When people from northern Europe settled in what is now the Guianas, the Spanish and Portuguese did not want the land badly enough to brave the forests and drive them out.

Today, this isolated and thinly populated area on the northeast coast belongs to the British, the French, and the Dutch. In the seventeenth century, what is now Surinam belonged to the British. But the British exchanged it for the Dutch possessions in the Hudson River Valley, which they had already seized. The Dutch were satisfied because they believed Surinam would be more profitable.

French Guiana is the smallest of the colonies, with an area of 28,000 square

In villages like this, Surinam's "bush Negroes" carry on the way of life of their African ancestors.

Jane M. Singer—Shostal

miles. Surinam is twice as big, and British Guiana is three times as big.

More than half the people of Surinam and British Guiana are Asian Indian and Javanese. The rest are Negroes, native Indians, and mixed peoples. The people of French Guiana are almost entirely Negro.

Most of the people in the Guianas are the descendants of slaves and laborers from Africa and Asia. They have been brought in over the years to make up for the lack of native Indians to work the plantations.

In all the Guianas nine tenths of the people live on one hundredth of the land, because the highlands are too rugged and isolated for settlement.

About half of French Guiana's 28,000 people live in its capital and only city, Cayenne. The population of Surinam is about a quarter of a million people. More than a third of them live in the capital, Paramaribo. British Guiana's population is twice as big as Surinam's. Most of these people live and work on the sugar cane plantations on the coast around New Amsterdam and Georgetown, the capital.

By far the most valuable resource of Surinam is bauxite (aluminum ore). It is also found in British Guiana, but Surinam is the world's largest producer.

Gold, diamonds, and manganese are mined in British Guiana and a little gold is found in French Guiana. The dense forests of Surinam contain rocks that promise to yield valuable minerals.

In Surinam there is a modern plywood factory and the government is mapping the forests in order to build up the lumber industry. In British Guiana there are many lumber mills which prepare the valuable timber of the highlands for shipment.

British Guiana's largest exports are raw sugar and the rum and molasses made from it. Surinam's main crop is rice. It also grows fruits and other food crops along the coast. In French Guiana the people grow only enough food to feed themselves. None is exported.

Fujihira—Monkmeyer

The natives of British Guiana travel up and down the rivers in long, slim dugout canoes.

Fritz Henle—Photo Researchers

Canal barges take sugar cane to the refinery in the marshy lowlands of British Guiana.

Freighters carry bauxite from British and Dutch Guiana to aluminum refineries in North America.

Fritz Henle—Photo Researchers

Fritz Henle—Photo Researchers

Shallow Lake Maracaibo's great oil field is tapped by oil derricks standing far out from shore.

Jerry Cooke—Photo Researchers

This brightly lighted Venezuelan oil refinery works a busy round-the-clock schedule.

Industries of Venezuela and Colombia

The first Spanish explorers of the region around Lake Maracaibo found Indian villages built on piles in the shallow water of the lake. This led them to call the region "Venezuela," or "Little Venice." The present-day country of Venezuela is over twice as large as California. But its population is less than half California's.

Colombia was named after Christopher Columbus. It is half again as big as Venezuela and has more than twice as many people.

Most of the people in both countries live in the highlands. In Colombia they occupy the narrow mountain valleys. The south-

Steel-helmeted workers come on shift at the Cerro Bolívar iron mine in eastern Venezuela.

Ernst Baumann—Birnback

eastern lowland which forms two thirds of the country is almost unoccupied. In Venezuela most people live in the Venezuelan Highlands, a continuation of the eastern chain of the Andes, the Cordillera de Mérida. The southern half of Venezuela is in the Guiana Highlands. It is also almost unoccupied.

The Venezuelan Highland rises sharply just south of the coast. The coast itself is very hot and dry, but the mountains are cool and have plenty of rain. Almost all the activity of the country is centered here.

In one valley of the coastal range is the lake of Valencia and the city of the same name. In another is the city of Caracas, Venezuela's capital. Over a million people live in Caracas. It has beautiful wide avenues. Its slums have been torn down to make parks. Its buildings are modern. It seeks to attract tourists by building magnificent new hotels. It is one of the most spectacular cities in the world.

Colombia's capital city, Bogotá, is also in the mountains, the eastern chain of the Andes. Even though it is very difficult to reach, this city is a center for writers, artists, and students.

In spite of the similarity of settlement in these two countries—thickly settled high-

Iron ore from Cerro Bolívar is loaded aboard oceangoing freighters at Puerto Ordaz, on the Orinoco River. From here it is shipped to steel mills in Pennsylvania and Alabama.

The mine at Paz del Río (below) supplies iron ore for Colombia's newly developed steel industry.

In Venezuela only half the people are farmers. Oil and other minerals make up more than 95 per cent of its exports.

Oil production is quite recent in Venezuela. The Indians who lived around Lake Maracaibo knew nothing of the value of the black, sticky stuff that sometimes spoiled their water and stuck to their fish nets. Then, in 1917, oil companies began drilling in and around their lake. The oil they found there has made Venezuela one of the largest oil producers in the world.

Since Lake Maracaibo is shallow, a refinery was built on the western side of the peninsula of Paraguana so that ocean ships could load oil. There is a pipeline connecting the refinery to the wells. Recently, the

Robert Leahey—Shostal

The new steel mill in Bogotá state, Colombia, sells all its steel within the country itself.

lands and almost unoccupied lowland areas —they are very different. Two thirds of the people in Colombia work at farming. The main export is coffee. Crops account for more than four fifths of Colombia's total exports.

The men in this pit are digging for emeralds. Colombia is famous for its fine emeralds.

Harrison Forman—Shostal

Roy Pinney—Photo Library

This dredge is being used to bring up gold-bearing rock from the bottom of the Atrato River.

lake has been dredged, and ships can get in to load oil, coffee, and other products of the region.

Northeast of Lake Maracaibo is the Segovia Highland. Until recently it has been a poor place, so dry that few people lived there. Now it has new roads and a huge oil refinery. A vast industrial center being built at Morón will make this area more prosperous.

Oil and natural gas have also been found on the Orinoco Llanos. The oil is piped to the coast and the gas to several cities nearby.

Colombia has found oil near the Venezuelan border and in the Magdalena River valley. This, too, goes to the coast through pipelines.

Until 1940 the heavily forested Guiana Highlands of Venezuela had been gone over only by explorers. Gold was found at Callao and the mine still operates.

But the real Highland development has been since World War II, when North American steel companies found a very rich grade of iron ore there. Now two private companies work mines along the Orinoco and Caroní Rivers. They have built roads and railroads, dredged shallow rivers, and built towns for workers with docks, warehouses, airports, and offices.

The Venezuelan government is building another steel industry of its own near Puerto Ordaz near the raw materials it needs.

In Colombia there is a new steel mill northeast of Bogotá. The land nearby contains almost all the materials needed for making steel.

There are emerald mines near Bogotá, too, but they are not worked steadily. The main mining district of Colombia is the thinly settled Atrato Valley in the northwest of the country near the Panamanian border, where gold and platinum are found. Colombia has been a world leader in the production of platinum for years. Now the Atrato Valley gold mines promise to be the best in South America.

Colombia's industry and trade are chiefly concentrated in the Antioquia region, in the central range of the Andes. The towns and cities of this region are built in the narrow valleys carved by the rivers. Travel is so difficult over the steep mountains that the region was formerly almost completely isolated from the rest of the country.

In their isolation, the Antioquians developed their own traditions of hard work and self-reliance. They worked their farms

Joe Barnell—Shostal

Medellín has modern textile mills. This girl is working at a loom which weaves vicuña wool.

themselves instead of relying on tenants and slaves. They later became Colombia's industrialists and businessmen.

The leading industry of Antioquia is textile weaving. It is centered around the city of Medellín. About half of the industrial workers are employed in textile plants. Among the other industries are drugs, chemicals, electrical appliances, and machinery.

These Antioquian bags are not pocketbooks, but shoulder bags carried by men of Medellín.

Joe Barnell—Shostal

The trampling hoofs of horses thresh wheat spread in a circle of stones in the Venezuelan Andes.

The Venezuelan government encourages Portuguese immigrants to establish farms.

Agriculture in Venezuela and Colombia

In Venezuela the Valley of Valencia and its slopes are the chief agricultural area. Sugar cane is grown in the lower parts. There is cotton for the textile factories of Valencia and Caracas. There is food for Venezuela's cities, and many dairy cattle. Coffee and cacao are grown on the estates of large landowners. The coffee is an especially good variety and it has become Venezuela's leading export crop.

Coffee is important to Venezuela because it can be grown on slopes which are too steep for most other uses, and it does not require much labor.

The owners of the large estates do not live there. The valley is low and hot. The owners stay in Caracas, where the height of the land makes living more comfortable.

The main coffee region of Venezuela is in the same mountain chain as that around

Valencia, the Cordillera de Mérida, but it is farther south and west. Here, the valleys are quite low and the mountains are so high that there is permanent snow on some of their peaks. Coffee is grown on the lower slopes, and other crops are planted according to height. There are roads connecting this region with many parts of the country.

Colombia's coffee trade started quite recently, but it has become very important to the country. Many of the trees are grown on the slopes of the eastern mountains on small plantations which are worked by their owners.

Another large coffee area is the Antioquia region. Here, also, the coffee is planted

Courtesy of the Pan American Coffee Bureau

When coffee berries turn cherry-red, they are ready for picking. Coffee beans are their seeds.

Colombian workers spread coffee beans in the sun to dry. Before roasting the beans are a pale color.

Annan Photo Features

In Colombia rice is grown in the highlands where the ground is dry, and large threshers are used.

An overseer watches over tenant workers cutting sugar cane on a plantation near Calí, Colombia.

on the mountain slopes and cared for by the people who own the land. It was coffee which first made Antioquia prosperous.

This region is very hard to reach because the land is so rugged. No road to the outside was built until 1955. But recently several roads and tunnels have been built to connect it to the coast. Airplanes carry passengers and some goods. But coffee, which is too bulky to carry cheaply by air, is still usually carried on muleback.

There are also large coffee plantations on the edge of the Magdalena Valley.

Large numbers of livestock are raised in Venezuela and Colombia. Cattle are pastured both in the hot lowlands and on the Alpine meadows of the mountains, where the cool climate is better for them.

The Orinoco Llanos would seem to be a natural cattle range because of its huge expanse of level grasslands. But conditions there are not suited to raising high-quality cattle. The native grasses are low in food value, and in the dry season they are too dry and hard to be eaten. In the wet season the cattle must wade or swim long distances to reach the islands of higher ground that are not flooded. Most of the year the cattle exist on the verge of starvation. Insects torment them and transmit disease.

Despite these natural disadvantages, herds of tough, scrawny cattle have ranged the Llanos for three hundred years. Recently, the Venezuelan government has begun to improve the cattle by cross-breeding and to introduce modern methods of insect control and better feed crops.

Bananas are grown on Colombia's northern coastal plain. They must be shipped while still green.

Annan Photo Features

After the rainy season, cattle in the Magdalena Valley are driven to graze near the river.

Problems of Transportation

Transportation has always been a big problem in both Venezuela and Colombia. The high mountains divide Colombia's people into isolated groups. They are just beginning to be able to communicate with one another.

In Venezuela road and railroad building has been so expensive that most goods were still carried on muleback until a few years ago. One of the first all-weather roads was built from La Guaira on the coast to Caracas in the mountains six miles away. To cover the six miles, the road had to wind upward for twenty-three miles over a mountain pass 3,400 feet high.

Beef from Orinoco Valley cattle is carried by air to Caracas over the highlands.

Charles Perry Weimer—House of Photography

Hamilton Wright Organization, Inc.

The great modern highway to Caracas, Venezuela, dwarfs the smaller, more winding roads near it.

Now a good road goes through the mountains instead of over them, by way of bridges and tunnels. Many other modern highways have taken the place of railroads.

Most of the highland settlements of Colombia use the Magdalena River as a route to the sea. Since it is very long and passes through some of the most productive areas in the country, it looks on the map like a good route for travel. But actually it is a difficult one. The mouth of the river keeps filling with sand. The sandbars and channels up the river shift constantly. There are impassable rapids at Honda.

But in spite of these difficulties, the river must be used because there is little other transportation. Where there are rapids, goods are sent around them overland. They are loaded again into ships after the rough parts are passed. Then they are carried to Cartagena and Baranquilla. Cartagena is connected to the river by a channel and with Medellín by an all-weather road.

Colombia is very advanced in its air travel. It was the first country in the western hemisphere to have a commercial airline. A trip from the Caribbean to the mountains which used to take from eight to thirty days now takes an hour and a half. Air travel is a real necessity in a country where every community is so isolated.

Venezuela has concentrated on building all-weather roads. It now has a considerable network of them and truck transportation has grown tremendously.

Steamers on the Magdalena River must move carefully between shifting sandbars and shoals.

Annan Photo Features

In Colombia many products are shipped by air over the impassable mountain peaks.

Roy Pinney—Photo Library

The volcanoes in Ecuador tower over the valleys. Their peaks are always wreathed in clouds.

THREE COUNTRIES OF THE ANDES

Along the entire western side of the South American continent runs a high range of mountains, the Andes. Ecuador, Peru and Chile are three of the countries included in this mountainous strip of land. Ecuador and Peru are divided by the Andes into three different kinds of land. There are the mountains themselves, the strip of lower land that goes all the way down the west coast, and the tropical valleys and lowlands east of the mountains.

Ecuador is the smallest of the Andes countries. It is about as big as Colorado. Peru is a little smaller than Alaska. Chile is as long from north to south as the whole width of the United States from coast to coast. Its average width is only about as far as from New York to Boston. Its total area is a little larger than that of Texas.

The mountains of Ecuador are so high that it is very difficult to cross them except by airplane. Even the mountain valleys are high. Many of them are as high as the peaks of our Rocky Mountains.

Scientists call the Andes new mountains, although they are about 60,000,000 years old. They are still being pushed up. A sign of this is that deep underground the earth is still moving and there are frequent earthquakes. Another sign is that many of the mountains are active volcanoes.

Some of Ecuador's thirty volcanoes are among the highest in the world. They may be quiet for as much as a century, then suddenly erupt. When they do, they cover the country around them with lava and ash. At night, the clouds which form around their tops glow with orange light reflected from the molten lava in their craters. The western slopes of these volcanoes are covered with deep ash carried by winds' blowing from the east.

Along the border between Ecuador and Peru, there is a pass in the mountains. Here, by climbing only 7,000 feet, you can get from the Pacific Ocean to the Amazon Valley. Imagine yourself climbing stairs to the top of a building 700 stories high. And this is one of the lowest passes in the mountains of Peru!

In very high places the air is thin. Breathing is not as easy as it is at sea level. Working—or playing—at great heights is difficult. People going to the mountains in Peru often get "mountain sickness" and feel dizzy and nauseated.

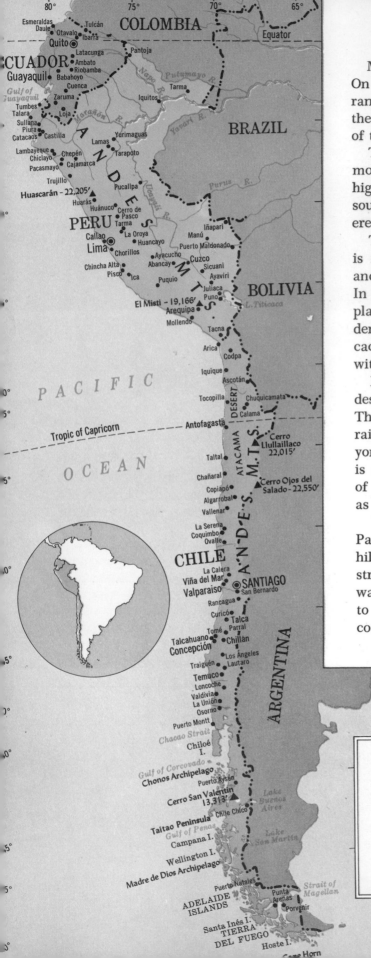

Much of Peru's highland is level plateau. On top of this high surface groups and ranges of enormous mountains rise as if they were piled on a table. Here, too, some of them are active volcanoes.

The Chilean Andes are high through most of their length. Just south of the highest mountains is the lake country of southern Chile. Here gigantic snow-covered volcanoes tower over the many lakes.

The eastern side of the Andes in Ecuador is rainy. The slopes are heavily forested and slant down toward the Amazon Valley. In Peru's east the land is also low. In many places the highlands drop down very suddenly to lowlands. Northeast of Lake Titicaca the land drops nearly 20,000 feet within about one hundred miles.

Many of the rivers beginning in the Andes flow into the Amazon River in Brazil. The constant rush of water has carved the rainy eastern slopes into ravines and canyons with sides so steep and straight that it is almost impossible to climb them. Some of these river beds are nearly twice as deep as the Grand Canyon.

The land west of the Andes, along the Pacific Ocean, starts in Ecuador with low hills and plains. The northern part of this strip is always wet and rainy, but southward toward Peru, there is a sudden shift to desert. On a small part of Peru's west coast, a few desert plants grow. Most of

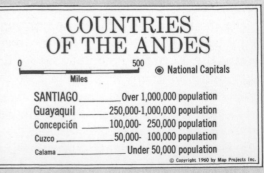

COUNTRIES OF THE ANDES

0 _____ 500
Miles   ◉ National Capitals

SANTIAGO _____ Over 1,000,000 population
Guayaquil _____ 250,000-1,000,000 population
Concepción _____ 100,000- 250,000 population
Cuzco _____ 50,000- 100,000 population
Calama _____ Under 50,000 population

© Copyright 1960 by Map Projects Inc.

Charles Perry Weimer—House of Photography

An Atacama Desert copper mine is surrounded by a vast expanse of barren, rolling sand.

Courtesy of Pan American World Airways

In the lake district of Chile, high mountains and active volcanoes tower over sparkling lakes.

the land, however, is completely bare and so dry that only its oases can be used for farming.

In northern Chile, just south of Peru, is the Atacama Desert. It is a vast strip of barren land stretching for six hundred miles between high mountains on the east and the lower plateaus of the coast on the west. It is one of the driest places on earth. There is one desert weather station at which no rain has ever been recorded! In the whole length of the desert, there is only one river, the Río Loa.

Along the edge of the sea, great rocky cliffs rise straight up as high as three-hundred-story buildings. Millions of years ago, when the land was lower, waves made terraces in the cliffs. Today towns cling to these rocky shelves over the sea. There are no harbors or even protected places along the northern part of Chile's coast.

The middle third of Chile is a beautiful strip of green land between the towering Andes and the sea. It is called the Central Valley. It is a land of thriving crops and fine trees. Streams from the Andes cross the valley and cut through the plateaus on the coast to reach the Pacific.

Much of this central coast is like the coast farther north. But here harbors are formed by points of land which jut out and protect ships from the southern winds.

The Central Valley goes as far south as Chile's lake district. Here forest takes the place of green pastureland and the climate is wetter and cooler.

The far south of Chile is very close to the Antarctic continent. It is one of the stormiest places in the world. Two thirds of the days every year have stormy, rainy weather. There are only about fifty days of sun. Glaciers, which start in the mountains, go all the way to the sea.

The coast is broken up into channels and islands. All the land is covered with soggy forest wherever there is enough soil for trees to grow. It is so wet here that the trees cannot be burned off to clear land. There is always wind, and the driving rain never stops. The outer islands are always pounded by heavy seas.

A winding stream cuts its way through the Andes in Peru, providing irrigation for valley farms.

George Hunter—Annan Photo Features

Land of the Incas

There are not as many people in the Andes countries as there are in similar regions in the United States. But many places are quite crowded because so much of the land cannot be utilized. Many of the four million people of Ecuador and the ten million people of Peru live in tight clusters in the valleys between high mountain peaks. Most of the rest live on the parts of the coast that are not too wet or too dry.

Nine tenths of the seven million people of Chile live in the middle third of the country. Nothing can be grown in the northern desert, and the stormy south is too wet.

In Ecuador and Peru about eight tenths of the people are pure Indian or mestizo (people with Indian and white ancestors). Most of them are descended from the Indians governed by the Incas. The Incas were rulers of a great Indian empire which was already five hundred years old when the Spanish explorers came to the Andes in the sixteenth century.

The Incas were skillful engineers. They paved their roads and suspended bridges across broad canyons. They made terraces on mountain slopes to keep water from washing the soil away. They brought water to dry places in irrigation ditches. They did not know about wheels, but somehow they brought ten-ton blocks of stone from far away to build their walls. These stones

Peruvian Indian children are accustomed to the thin air of the high mountains.

Eric Pavel—FLO

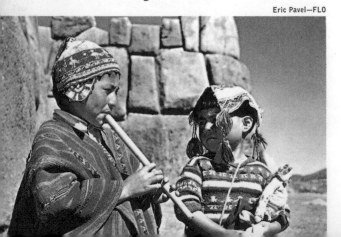

were fitted so closely that a knife blade cannot be stuck between them. The walls have stood firm through earthquakes that toppled modern buildings.

The Incas designed beautiful pottery and cloth and made exquisite objects of gold and silver. Although they had no system of writing, they kept accounts with knots by a decimal system they invented. They knew a great deal about the stars.

The vast Inca empire reached from northern Ecuador to middle Chile. It included many tribes the Incas had conquered. The centers of the empire were at Quito, Ecuador, and Cuzco, Peru.

The government controlled an amazing number of subjects, probably between sixteen and thirty million. The people were told where to live, what to plant, how much to work, even whom to marry. The emperor owned everything and distributed it as a father might to small children. He cared for his people's needs, solved their problems and demanded that they obey him.

When the Spaniards took over the empire, the people were so accustomed to having their lives run for them that the Spaniards seemed to them only a slightly different group of rulers.

In Chile the Araucanian Indians were rather like our Iroquois. They did some farming as they moved from place to place, but mostly they were hunters and fishers. The northern Araucanian tribes were conquered by the Incas. The southern tribes, who lived in the woods, fought among the trees so well that they were never conquered. One group of Araucanians in middle Chile learned about irrigation from the Incas and became farmers, but they remained fiercely independent. The best and bravest Spanish soldiers were sent to conquer these Indians and many of them married Araucanian women. These people were the ancestors of the mestizos of middle Chile today. About two thirds of the people of Chile are mestizo. Most of the rest are white.

Macchu Picchu was a lost city built before the time of the Incas. It has only recently been rediscovered.

Ernst Baumann—Birnback

In Ecuador slopes as high as 10,000 feet are plowed and used for growing highland crops.

Farming in the Andes

The Indians of Ecuador and Peru are mostly very poor farmers who live in valleys high in the mountains. They are separated from the rest of the world by almost impassable ranges and peaks.

Farming in mountains as high as the Andes presents problems we do not face in North America. Here, we plant crops where they will grow best. What we do not use, we send to market over our network of roads and railroads. In the Andes the ruggedness of the land makes it so hard to send anything away that farmers grow only what food they can use themselves. And they must grow it where it *will* grow, not where it grows best.

Certain foods will grow up to certain heights and no higher, so planting on slopes is done according to elevation. Potatoes will grow highest of all, up to 14,000 feet. The next highest crop is barley. Wheat grows somewhat lower, then corn and alfalfa up to 11,000 feet. Cotton and sugar cane are grown in the lower valleys.

Only cattle are sold outside. They can be driven down the mountain trails, but they become thin on the trip and must be fattened in lowland pastures before they are sold.

Many of the Indian farmers are tenants. They are the descendants of the Inca people the Spanish used as slaves. They work for the owners of large private estates who are the descendants of the first Spanish conquerors. The farmers are no longer slaves, but poverty makes life hard for many of them.

An Indian tenant farmer must clear the forest and grow his own corn high on the slope of a mountain. The better land farther down is used by the landowner himself, often for grazing cattle.

Other Indians work their own land, or farm in groups much as they did during the Inca Empire. They know almost nothing about modern farming. Some use small foot plows instead of plows drawn by oxen —or even hoes. Grain is winnowed by tossing it in the wind, or threshed by animals trampling it on a threshing floor.

In primitive parts of Peru, potatoes are planted much as they were in the days of the Incas.

There are a few commercial farms in the mountains of Peru. The food is not sent down to the coast, but sold to mountain mining towns nearby.

Cattle can graze in the mountains where the land is too high for anything to grow but grass. There are some slopes, especially in Peru, that are too high even for cattle. These are used for grazing sheep, alpacas, llamas, and vicuñas. Indian shepherds care for the flocks as high as 17,000 feet up the mountains. The wool is sent to the coast for the owners, and the shepherds live off the flocks, which supply them with meat, clothing, and fuel.

The people of the low west coast of Ecuador are mostly Negro. They raise bananas, coffee, and rice on their small farms. The Negro farmers were the first to grow bananas in this area. Now bananas are Ecuador's biggest export crop, but shipping them is difficult and expensive; so the banana business is not very profitable.

They are carried by mules or porters to trucks. The trucks take them to river boats or barges. They are loaded by hand, then taken out to big ships. The ships cannot go into the ports because the water is too shallow.

The few Indians in this region raise some cacao and gather tagua nuts for making imitation ivory. But their main industry is in Chone, where Panama hats are made from a special straw they gather in the forests.

Tossing the wheat in the air, an ancient method, allows the wind to blow away the chaff.

A herd of llamas passes a series of ancient Incan irrigation terraces cut into the mountain slopes.

The most valuable cropland in Ecuador is the lowland northeast of Guayaquil. It is hot and humid, but the soil is rich and there are no strong winds. Coffee and rice are grown here. New land is cleared for each crop instead of enriching it and planting it again. This wasteful method is gradually destroying much of the land in South America.

It is hard to believe that the strip of barren desert on the west coast of Peru could be good farmland, but fine crops are grown there. Along the coast are forty oases, like green stripes across the dry land. Streams flowing down the mountains cross the desert to the coast. Their water is used to irrigate the land. Some of the streams have cut such deep canyons that the water must be taken far upstream from the oases where it is used.

Little railway engines pull loads of bananas on flatcars through a plantation in Ecuador.

In this cool, dry, cloudy place cotton, sugar cane, and rice are grown. And in the middle section there are also vineyards and vegetable farms to supply Peru's cities.

Peru's cool coastal climate is caused by a cold ocean current that sweeps by the shore from the south. This current is full of fish. The fish are eaten by millions of sea birds which nest on the offshore islands. The birds' manure, preserved by the dry climate, makes a valuable fertilizer called guano.

The landowners of middle Chile are much closer to their land and their tenants than most other South American landowners. They live on their haciendas instead of in cities. Many of them have as much Indian blood as their tenants.

The tenant on a Chilean hacienda lives on land which once belonged to his ancestors. Now it belongs to the owner, but the tenant still feels that the mud-walled house and small lot given him by the owner are his permanent home. He may work in primitive ways, but the soil is rich and the harvest is good.

The tenant grows food for his family and often a little extra wheat to sell. The owner usually raises cattle and cattle feed. He, too, plants wheat. Chile is the only country in South America where the people grow more wheat than corn. On small farms there are often fruits and olives instead of grains. Chile does not grow enough food to feed her population, and must import large amounts every year.

Grapes grow particularly well in the Central Valley. Almost every farm and hacienda has vineyards. Some of them are very large. The raisins and wine made from Chilean grapes are famous. They are sold to North America and Europe as well as within South America.

The hacienda system is changing in Chile. Many of the large estates are being divided and sold to small farmers. Some of the farm workers have pushed southward to cut farms out of the dense forests. They were led by small groups of Germans who opened the frontier and built strong, permanent homes and all-weather roads. Many trees must be cleared to build farms here. The wood is used for fuel rather than lumber.

Sea birds of the islands off the coast of Peru are so numerous that they blacken the sky in flight.

Joe Barnell—Shostal

Food production is increased in Chile by planting potatoes between rows of grape vines.

Rosene—Shostal

Mining and Industry

Four fifths of Ecuador's people and most of its occupied land are devoted to farming and cattle. But there are minerals in Ecuador. Although the Spaniards did not find it, there is gold near Esmeraldas. There is an oil field west of Guayaquil. And there are probably other minerals to be discovered in the mountains and in the empty land east of them.

Peru's land and people are also agricultural, but not as much so as Ecuador's. Peru is working at improving roads and railroads. Being able to ship goods from one part of the country to another is sure to lead to more industry and more prosperity.

Copper and iron ore are produced near Peru's west coast, but the chief mining towns are high in the mountains. In the 1600's a huge supply of silver was found near Cerro de Pasco. The silver mines were worked for hundreds of years. The silver was melted out of the ore and made into rough bars. The bars were carried over a steep trail down 15,000 feet and over two hundred miles to Lima.

Eventually, the ore began to give out and the mines were hardly worked. But early in this century a mining company took over the area to exploit other minerals. It built an amazing railroad up the mountains from Lima. It goes over bridges and along shelves cut out of sheer rock walls. It winds through spiral tunnels hollowed inside mountains and up zig-zag inclines to get to the mining country. The railroad was very expensive to build, but it has been worthwhile to be able to carry equipment to the mines and minerals to Lima.

Many valuable minerals have been discovered in the mines around Cerro de Pasco. There are gold, lead, zinc, and bismuth. There are new veins of silver. But the most important mineral in Peru is copper, Peru's second export.

The Spanish sent workers to the mines from lower places, but the thin air was very bad for them. The mining companies have taught the people of the highlands to do the skilled work. These workers are

In a Peruvian mountain valley 15,000 feet high, this mine produces tin, gold, silver, lead and zinc.

Ores mined nearby are processed in these smelters at Cerro de Pasco. The work is done by skilled Indians.

accustomed to high altitudes and are able to work better.

Coal has been found near Cerro de Pasco. This is important because South America has so little. There seems to be enough so that Peru may become South America's leading producer of coal.

There is oil in the northwest tip of Peru, along the coast. The oil is refined for export at Talara.

An oil refinery at Talara, Peru, processes oil from several fields in the north of Peru.

Hamilton Wright Organization, Inc.

Water is pumped to dry lakes of the Atacama in order to extract chemicals from the nitrate beds.

Much of Chile's prosperity has come from the Atacama Desert. In colonial days the desert was only a travel route. Its only inhabitants were Indians who lived in tiny settlements at the foot of the Andes on the eastern edge of the desert. These settlements were so hard to find that lighthouses were built to guide travelers to them.

The first minerals to be exploited in the desert were silver and copper. The prospectors who searched for these metals also found deposits of sodium nitrate in the dried-up lake beds of the desert.

When nitrate was found to be excellent fertilizer, a nitrate industry started which made Chile prosperous. When nitrate was found valuable for explosives, the resulting demand started a war. The northernmost deposits lay in the area where the borders of Chile, Peru, and Bolivia came together. But these borders had never been clearly agreed upon. Now each country claimed the land.

The war began in 1879 and continued for four years. When peace finally came, Peru had lost its part of the Atacama. Bolivia was left with no nitrate and no seacoast. And Chile owned all the nitrate.

The nitrate boom ended when a way was found to extract nitrogen from the air. Now the Atacama supplies only one tenth of the world's nitrate. Iodine is a by-product.

The open-pit copper mine at Chuquicamata, Chile, is one of the largest in the world.

Courtesy of ANACONDA

Herbert Lanks—Monkmeyer

Most of the exports from Chile's fertile Middle Valley go through the seaport of Valparaíso.

The many workers of the nitrate industry depend entirely on nitrate for a living. If there should be no need for them any longer, whole towns would disappear.

Chile's largest mineral export today is copper. Most of it comes from three copper mines high in the Andes in the Atacama region. Chile also has coal and enough iron ore to supply itself with steel. Sulfur is found in the Andes, too, but it is very hard to get, so Chile does not export very much. The deposits are inside the craters of enormously high volcanoes. Some sulfur is brought out, but it is difficult for the workers to get into the craters, and they have a hard time breathing in the thin air. Gold, silver, and other metals are also produced.

Ecuador has very little industry of any kind. Panama hats are made in several cities and in the capital, Quito, are factories which make cloth and leather goods.

Lima, the capital, has long been Peru's center of government, social life, and business. Lately it has also become a center of industry. Its many small factories make such things as foods and cloth, soap and cigarettes, leather goods and matches.

About sixty per cent of Chile's people live in cities, and the cities are growing fast. Santiago, the capital of Chile, is a sprawling mass of new buildings and factories which dwarf the original Spanish city.

Valparaíso, the port of Santiago, was built on the coast, at the foot of a steep slope. As the city grew, it crept up the slope. Now there are many places where people ride in elevators instead of buses to get from one neighborhood to another.

Concepcion and Valdivia are also becoming centers of industry. Many farm workers are moving to the cities to work in the new factories.

The industries of middle Chile use raw materials from many parts of Chile. Grapes come from the vineyards nearby. Wool is sent down the steep mountain slopes to the textile factories. The tanneries get hides from mountain cattle. Grains are made into flour and beer. In Valdivia there are furniture factories using wood from local forests. A new steel industry is beginning and many more workers will soon be working in steel plants.

The Far South

Tierra del Fuego is an island at the tip of the South American continent. When Ferdinand Magellan sailed with his fleet through the channel which is now called the Strait of Magellan, he saw constant flickering fires on the island shore. He called the island "Land of Fire" because of the mysterious lights. Magellan did not know it, but the lights were the fires of the Indians. They kept them burning constantly because they did not know how to kindle new fire.

The far south is a place of snow-capped mountains and glaciers, of storms and high waves. The weather is so forbidding here that one of Magellan's ships refused to go further and turned back.

On Tierra del Fuego is the town of Ushuaia, the southernmost town in the world. But a more important city is Punta Arenas, where most of the South's activity centers.

Punta Arenas is on the small part of Chile that is east of the Andes. Here the mountains provide shelter from the constant wind and rain. Sheep are raised north of the city. They now number two million.

Across the strait, on Tierra del Fuego, oil was discovered during World War II. Now there are one hundred wells in an area that was almost completely without population a generation ago.

Ushuaia in Argentine Tierra del Fuego is the southernmost permanent town in the world.

Patrice Hartley—Rapho Guillumette

Eric Pavel—FLO

Cattle are brought to this part of the Argentine pampa to be fattened before they are sold.

THE SOUTHERN COUNTRIES

Southern South America is the region south of the Brazilian Highlands and east of the Andes. It is mountainous on the west, but large areas are covered by an almost flat plain called the *pampa*. This fertile plain is the great wheat-growing and cattle-raising region of South America.

The northeast portion is a land of gently rolling hills and abundant rainfall. Summers here are hot and the winters are mild. Both temperature and rainfall decrease as one goes south. The southern plateau of Patagonia is a cold, dry, barren desert. The few people that live in this stormy land are sheep raisers.

Rainfall also decreases as you travel inland, for the Andes shut off rain-bearing winds from the west, and virtually all rain has to come from the Atlantic Ocean. A dry belt runs from north to south between the mountains and the well-watered eastern region.

Two countries occupy this region—Argentina and Uruguay. Although Uruguay,

Tom Hollyman—Photo Researchers

A group of Argentine gauchos prepares to cook the evening meal over a fire on the pampa.

which was once part of Brazil, is the smallest independent country in South America, and Argentina the second largest, they have a great deal in common.

Both countries have populations which are almost entirely white, with most of the people of Spanish or Italian ancestry. In Argentina, with the exception of the relatives of Japanese who already live there, immigration has been restricted to white peoples.

In both countries the most important industries are stock-raising and agriculture, especially the raising of grain for cattle and for export.

And both Argentina and Uruguay are more prosperous than the average South American country. In fact, Uruguay is claimed to be the only South American country which protects its agricultural laborers with a minimum wage law. This, of course, raises the general standard of living.

Publicolor—Shostal

This green valley in Argentina is in the beautiful lake district of the southern Andes.

On a sheep ranch in dry, windswept Patagonia, water is pumped by a windmill.

Joe Barnell—Shostal

Argentina

Argentina is the biggest country in South America after Brazil. Its million square miles and twenty million people are a sixth of the land and a sixth of the population of the continent. Unlike most South Americans, Argentines are accustomed to prosperity. Most of the people can read and write, and only about a quarter of them work on farms.

Ninety-seven per cent of the people in Argentina are white. There are almost no Negroes and the mestizo population is mostly along the borders of surrounding countries.

The western border of Argentina is mostly in the Andes. It is very dry in the north, but further south there are oases in the foothills near the Sierra de Córdoba. The plains around Córdoba, where beef cattle graze now, were once breeding places for pack mules. In the eighteenth century as many as 60,000 mules were traded for silver every year at the fair at Salta.

Art D'Arazien—Shostal

Cattle ranges in Argentina's dry northwest depend on streams from the Andes for irrigation.

Tucumán was once a fortress at the southern end of the great Inca road from Cuzco in the Andes. It later became an outfitting center for travelers going east and west. Now it is the center of Argentina's sugar district.

Although the land at the edges of the Tucumán area is too cold or too dry for sugar, the district itself is protected by mountains and has a warm climate with enough rain and no frost.

South of Tucumán are the oases of the dry belt. Wherever rivers come down to the desert from the mountains, the land is irrigated. Many Italians live in the settlements around these oases. The largest are San Juan, Mendoza, and San Rafael. Their biggest trade crop is grapes. In Mendoza there are big wineries which make wine from the grapes of all the oasis vineyards.

Some oil fields have been found along the eastern edges of the Andes. And there are a few tiny mining communities in the northwest. The most important mineral there is asbestos. Argentina produces enough in this region to supply the whole United States.

Teams of mules guided by their riders pull the plows on an Argentine sugar cane plantation.

Joe Barnell—Shostal

Art D'Arazien—Shostal

Vineyard workers pick grapes at Mendoza. The snow-covered Andes tower behind them.

its course so often at flood time that the border is constantly shifting. Cotton is planted on some of the shifting flood plains after the land has dried.

The scrub forests of the Chaco contain millions of quebracho trees, which yield tannin for tanning leather. Their lumber is also used for products which require very hard wood, such as telephone poles and railroad ties.

The mills which extract the tannin need a great deal of water and must be built near rivers. All logging is done along the railroads that lead to the rivers. There are also cotton farmers on the quebracho land.

Art D'Arazien—Shostal

This winery makes wines from the grapes grown in most of the Argentine oases near the Andes.

The Argentine Mesopotamia (which means "between the rivers") is the region between the Paraná and Uruguay Rivers. It is rolling, green country, covered with woodland. Where the Paraná and Iquassú Rivers drop over the edge of the flat Paraná Plateau are the magnificent Guiara and Iquassú Falls.

Northern Mesopotamia is cattle land. In the south is one of Argentina's biggest sheep and flax districts. Yerba maté is cultivated in the far north. Maté, a popular beverage in Argentina, Uruguay, and Brazil, is made from the leaves of a small tree of the holly family. The population of the maté plantations is quite small during most of the year, but at harvest time people pour into the area from as far away as Brazil and Paraguay to gather maté leaves.

The Gran Chaco is an enormous, thinly settled lowland, shared by Argentina, Bolivia, and Paraguay. The Argentine part is covered with scrub woodland and grass. In the east the rivers flood in the summer, covering vast areas with water. The Pilcomayo River, which marks the boundary between Argentina and Paraguay, changes

People come from far away to harvest maté leaves, from which a popular beverage is made.

Eric Pavel—FLO

Heavy quebracho logs are loaded onto carriers by primitive methods, then hauled by oxen.

Straggling cattle graze beside a stream on the vast stretches of Argentina's western pampas.

They are mostly squatters who clear land or move in after the woodcutters have cleared it.

The dry southern part of Argentina is called Patagonia. Only one per cent of Argentina's people live there. There are constant stormy winds which whip up waves on the lakes at the foot of the Andes. Spectacular mountains are covered with glacial ice. Water can be found in the deep canyons that cross the dry plateaus, so that is where almost everyone in Patagonia lives.

The sheep ranches are enormous. They cover thousands of square miles and usually have headquarters in a canyon near water. Sheep are also raised on Tierra del Fuego near Ushuaia.

The pampas are the southern part of the great Argentine plains. The Dry Pampa, where rainfall is scanty, is on the west and south. The Humid Pampa is on the east.

The Humid Pampa is a boundless plain. It was covered with tall, rustling grass when the early explorers came. The winters are mild and the summers are hot. The

Gerard Oppenheimer—Alpha

Newly sheared sheep are gathered near the head-quarters of a Patagonian sheep ranch.

Wallace Litwin—Photo Researchers

Fine horses are bred and raised on the plains near Buenos Aires.

rainfall is plentiful. The growing season is longer in the north than in the south and west.

This entire area, except for a few hills, is covered with deep, fertile soil. It is made of dust blown from the dry west and south and of silt carried down by the rivers. There is not a stone or a pebble anywhere.

The early settlements were all cattle, horse, and sheep ranches on the rim of the Pampa in the northeast. The rest of the land, which now produces more food than almost any other region in the world, was used only for grazing. It was useless for agriculture until the beginning of modern farm methods.

When Argentina started shipping meat out of the country, it found people did not like the tough beef from native cattle. The ranchers began breeding fine British cattle. These were not as hardy as native cattle and they needed to have food grown for them.

The workers to grow feed crops came from Italy, Spain, and many other countries. Some of the tenants planted their own wheat and eventually wheat became a very

John Strohm

These cattle are bred from prime English stock brought into Argentina in the 19th century.

important crop. More workers were needed. For a number of years workers came from Italy for the Argentine harvest, then returned home for the Italian harvest. They were called "swallows" because of their yearly migration.

Roads on the Pampa are hard to keep passable. When there is no grass, the fine

The small wooden box travels up a cable to a large bin with its load of corn.

Sunflower harvesters go through the fields near Buenos Aires, picking the flowers and seeds.

dirt blows away in the dry seasons and turns to deep mud when it is wet. But building railroads on such level ground is simple. Railroads fan out from all the Pampa ports into the agricultural land, covering far more territory than the all-weather roads.

The Humid Pampa today is divided into four agricultural regions. In the east, beef cattle and sheep for wool and mutton are raised. Butter has become an important product.

The entire western and southern part is devoted to wheat, alfalfa and cattle. This is the area that borders on the Dry Pampa.

The corn region in the north around Rosario is thickly settled by a large number of Italians. Surrounding Buenos Aires, there is a region of vegetable and fruit farming. It is so concentrated that some of the gardens reach into the edges of the city.

Eric Pavel—FLO

In Buenos Aires' harbor the mud must be dredged constantly and held back by a wall.

Buenos Aires was chosen as a place for a colony because it had water deep enough for boats to come up close to the land. With the growth of the Humid Pampa it has become the biggest city in Latin America. The water is far too shallow for modern ships, and channels must be dug and constantly maintained to keep the port open. In 1935 an entirely new port was built directly north of the old one.

Argentina leads all the countries of South America in trade. It lacks oil, coal, and steel. But it ships almost all the wheat, linseed, and corn, most of the meat, and more than half of the wool, hides, grains, and wood that leave the continent. In fact, it is the world's leading exporter of fresh meat.

Hides are unloaded at a Buenos Aires tannery. The bales hold wool for textile factories.

Art D'Arazien—Shostal

Doris Jacoby—Shostal

These Uruguayan gauchos herd horses. Much land in Uruguay is used for horse and cattle raising.

Doris Jacoby—Shostal

Montevideo's modern hotels and the beautiful beaches near the city attract many vacationers.

A new hydroelectric power plant 150 miles from Montevideo supplies much of the city's power.

Julien Bryan—Photo Researchers

Uruguay

The 2,800,000 people of Uruguay occupy the smallest South American republic. There are only about 68,000 square miles of land. But Uruguay is the only country in South America in which none of the land is empty. The capital is Montevideo. The Uruguayans are mostly white people of Spanish and Italian descent. There are small numbers of other Europeans and a few Negroes. Near the borders there are some mestizos. The people are prosperous. Most of them can read and write.

The country is in the region where the plateaus of Brazil descend to the Humid Pampa of Argentina. A strip along the eastern Uruguay shore and the shore of the Plata River is low, but most of the country is hilly. There is none of the vast plain of the pampas, but grassy slopes and forested valleys. The coldest months are not very cold and the warmest months are not too hot for comfort. There is enough rain all through the year.

For almost two hundred years after the Spaniards arrived at the Plata River, Uruguay was occupied only by gauchos and their herds of wild cattle. Spain and Portugal had disputes about the land, but neither country settled it, or even set up ranch headquarters. The gauchos fought for Spain or Portugal, whoever paid the most. When no one paid, they fought each other.

The first settlements on the Plata shore

were made by Argentine cattle buyers who grew weary of following the herds all over the country. Ranches spread and permanent workers were hired. The gauchos were pushed back into the far parts of the country.

British businessmen were the first to realize that the grasslands of Argentina and Uruguay were valuable. In 1840, they imported fine sheep for wool. In ten years there were about two million sheep raised in Uruguay.

Until the 1860's the millions of cattle on Uruguay's unfenced pastures had been used only for tallow, hides, and salt beef. Fresh meat could not be kept cool for shipment.

Then Britain opened a meat processing company. Barbed wire fences made it possible to separate cattle for scientific breeding. Refrigerator ships made it possible to ship frozen meat to other countries. Fine cattle from Britain replaced Uruguayan range cattle.

Today Uruguay has more cattle and sheep in proportion to people than any other country in the world. About four fifths of the land is used for grazing. The rest is agricultural land in the south.

Uruguay's railroad system is now owned by the government, although it was built by the British and still uses British trains and coal. Gravel-surfaced roads have been built recently, and trucks and buses take care of much of the transportation of the country.

Montevideo is the center of commerce, government, and, recently, of industry. It is also the fishing port for the South Atlantic fishing fleet and a very popular resort. Electric power comes from a power plant on the Río Negro and from a steam-electric plant in the city which runs on imported coal. There are many manufacturing plants, using mostly local materials.

The government owns Montevideo's hotels and casinos and collects a good income from tourists, many of whom are from Argentina.

Julien Bryan—Photo Researchers

This Uruguayan truck-farmer raises vegetables and potatoes for the city markets.

It is unusual for a country in which almost half the workers are farmers or ranchers to be prosperous. Uruguay's government-owned industries are run to produce goods and services at low prices for everyone. The great majority of houses have telephones, gas, and electricity. Food is low priced, so that Uruguayans eat well. There is free medical service, health insurance, old age pensions, and many other benefits. Workers have an eight-hour day. Newspapers are not controlled by the government. All adults can vote.

Most of this high standard of living came about because of a remarkable president. His name was José Batlle y Ordóñez. Although he died in 1929, his influence is still felt. The idea he worked toward was: "It is not necessary that the rich should be made poorer, but only that the poor should be made less poor."

These sheep are in an open field, but Uruguay builds fenced runways for them in settled areas.

Joe Barnell—Shostal

BRAZIL—GIANT OF SOUTH AMERICA

Half the people in South America are Brazilians. The United States of Brazil is bigger than the United States of America without Alaska. Its population is only about one third as large as the population of the United States. Its land is as big as all the other South American countries combined. There are twenty states, a federal district, and five territories.

Brazil is the only country of South America where the official language is Portuguese and not Spanish.

The people of Brazil live almost entirely on or near the east coast. Most of the northern and western land is very thinly settled.

Brazil has more potential agricultural land than any other country of its size. It has the most magnificent natural harbor in the world. It has the longest navigable river in the world. The resources of its forests are endless and it is known to have great stores of iron ore and manganese.

All this should make many people want to live in Brazil. They might be expected to spread out over the country to take advantage of its riches. But this is not so. One of the reasons is that Brazil's riches are so poorly arranged for use by man.

The land that faces the sea on much of the east coast is made up of steep cliffs. These cliffs are especially steep behind Brazil's two largest cities, São Paulo and Rio de Janeiro with its great harbor. Most of the rivers rise in the highlands back of the coast, but instead of running directly toward the sea, they wander off to the north or south for hundreds of miles to join the Amazon or Paraná Rivers. This makes them useless for travel to or from the Atlantic Ocean.

The longest navigable river in the world, the Amazon, wanders endlessly through the great forests of valuable trees. It might be a route for shipping the wealth of the

Tropical Recife is a seaport named after the coral reef which shelters its spacious harbor.

Charles Perry Weimer—House of Photography

forest to the Atlantic coast. But the trees and plants are scattered all over the tremendous river valley, and too few people live along the river to gather them. So the Amazon, on which small ships can sail from the Atlantic almost across the continent, is of limited use as a means of travel and shipping.

The iron and manganese deposits are not near the coal needed to process them. Most of Brazil's high waterfalls, where power plants could be built, are far from where the power is needed, so it is difficult to establish these industries.

The levels of land in Brazil are not as varied as they are in the Andes countries. There are three areas of plains. The largest is the Amazon plain in the northwest. It narrows as the river goes toward the Atlantic Ocean.

There is a smaller lowland around the Paraguay River in the south. And there are very small bits of lowland along the Atlantic coast.

Harold Schultz—Birnback

Water buffalo pull a flatboat on a swampy part of Marajó Island in the mouth of the Amazon.

James R. Simon

Fishermen along the coast from Recife to the Amazon sail in woven boats with huge sails.

No traffic disturbs these children playing in the street in Cuiaba, in Brazil's far interior.

Len Sirman—Birnback

Most of the country is highland—the Brazilian Highlands, south of the Amazon, and the Guiana Highlands in the north. Both highlands are ancient plateaus, worn in places into rounded hills, with deeply cut river valleys. There are only a few mountain ranges above the high surface. The highest are the mountains northeast of Rio de Janeiro and those in the Guiana Highlands. There is a steep slope along the east coast called the "Great Escarpment." It is scarcely notched by rivers so there are no easy passages to the interior.

There are many kinds of climate in Brazil. They are not extreme as to heat and cold or rainfall and drought. Brazil is rainy and hot along most of the north coast and part of the east coast. It is rainy and cool in the south. There is no very cold season. The only dry, hot place is in the northeast, near the equator. In the far south there is occasional frost and snow.

Brazil suffers from a system of farming called "land rotation." The country is so enormous that forests can be cleared, crops or pastures planted and used for several years, then abandoned for newly cleared land. There is no fertilizing to prepare the land for the next crop.

This unwillingness to improve the land so it can be used every year has destroyed much of the good farmland in the country. The soil is washing off the slopes because the trees have been cleared and there are no roots left to hold it. In some flat places, the land has been cleared and used so often without refertilizing it that it will no longer grow anything.

These things often happen in pioneer lands, where the settlers believe that their natural resources are inexhaustible and do not take care of them. They happened in the United States long ago when it was still a pioneer country. As Brazil's population increases, and good land is no longer easily available, Brazilians will probably learn to take better care of their farmland. Until then, erosion will continue.

In Brazil's southernmost state, Rio Grande do Sul, most people live in the valleys and lowlands.

170

The Amazon jungle, often so dense that travel through it is impossible, crowds to the edge of the river.

Brazil's Northland— the Amazon

The Amazon country of Brazil is a land of forests and rivers. In the west the Amazon Plain is eight hundred miles wide. It narrows as it passes between the Brazilian and Guiana Highlands, then fans out again at the Atlantic coast. Where the river reaches the ocean, there is no lacework of streams because the land sinks gradually into the sea at this point, forming a great and extensive bay.

The floodplain (the area covered by the river at high water) of the Amazon is twenty to sixty miles wide on both sides. It is bordered by steep bluffs. Some of the silt carried down from the mountains by the floods of the wettest seasons collects along the river. This makes the soil very rich. But this area is so often flooded that farmers cannot make much use of it.

Many people think of the tropical Amazon climate as unbearably hot. Actually, the temperatures are not unusually high.

Freighters are able to travel far up the Amazon, even to the foothills of the Andes.

Harold Schultz—Birnback

Indians of the Amazon Valley live as they have for hundreds of years, untouched by civilization.

There is more difference between night and day than between summer and winter. It is the dampness that is uncomfortable.

There is no dry season, only a less wet season. There are sudden, hard showers and just as sudden clearings during the day in both seasons. The nights are almost always brilliant and clear.

In the huge Amazon forest are thousands of trees and shrubs, but they rarely grow in stands of one kind. The value of some of the trees is tremendous. There are all kinds of palms, hardwoods, dyewoods, medicinal plants, rubber, fruits, nuts, and gourds. But they are so scattered throughout the dense forest that it is difficult to exploit them.

What the forest lacks is people. It is one of the largest thinly populated places in the world. For example, Alaska is thinly populated, but there are about two people to a square mile. In the Amazon Valley there is only one person to every two square miles. And half of these live near the east coast.

Ever since the Amazon River and its forest were discovered, the men who have tried to gather its wealth have been hampered by the lack of workers.

The isolated groups of Indians in the forest fear and avoid white men. The early explorers taught them this fear. They brought disease and sold the Indians into slavery. Today's descendants of these Indians hunt and fish. They raise a few plants in jungle clearings which they abandon when they move on.

This huge opera house at Manaus was built during the prosperous days of the Amazon rubber boom.

Rubber gatherers in the Amazon jungle smoke the latex in huts until it can be formed into a ball.

Most homes in Manaus are small floating houses built on rafts. A dugout canoe serves as transportation.

A group of poverty-stricken families near Santarém is all that is left of a migration of North American slave-owners after the Civil War. They moved to South America, bringing their tools and their slaves with them, because they did not want to live without the slave system. They cleared the forest and planted cotton and sugar cane, but the cost of shipping from their isolated colony was so high that their venture failed.

The rubber trees of the Amazon forest have had the largest effect on its population. When the world began to want rubber in the middle of the nineteenth century, Brazil owned most of the wild rubber in the world. Everyone rushed to buy land along the Amazon, then set out on a frantic search for laborers. Indians from the eastern side of the Andes, where the law did not reach, were seized and enslaved. Workers came from the drought area in the east at a rate of 20,000 a year.

Brazil nuts are gathered from scattered trees in the jungle and loaded into ships at Belém.

The rubber owners got rich in the traditionally careless way of boom regions. They collected the rubber, but they made no effort to plant new trees or improve the land. They would take their workers up the river by boat and leave them to build shelters and cut paths to the rubber trees. Then they would come back from time to time to collect the rubber the workers had gathered. The owners paid the workers low wages, then sold them supplies at such high prices that the workers always owed them money.

Most of the towns along the Amazon today were originally bases from which the owners could control what went up and down the river. The biggest boom towns were Belém and Manaus. The increase in the rubber harvest was tremendous. It went from 70,000 pounds in 1827 to 5,200,000 pounds in 1853.

The rubber boom in Brazil was ended when an Englishman smuggled seeds out of the country and started rubber plantations in Malaya and Sumatra. The trees on the Asian plantations yielded three to six times as much rubber as those growing wild in the Amazon forest. And the workers could gather three times as much when the trees were all in one place. In thirty years Malaya and Sumatra were producing on these well-organized plantations most of the world's rubber. Brazil's business had declined to almost nothing.

Most of the families sprinkled up and down the Amazon are left over from the rubber boom. Many towns have been abandoned, swallowed up by the forest. Now Syrian traders have taken up where the rubber owners left off. They travel up and down the river in launches, picking up the gums, nuts, roots, woods, and skins gathered for them by the people of the tiny, poor communities that are dotted along the river's course.

Brazil produces most of the Brazil nuts in the world. But the nuts are gathered from wild trees, not cultivated ones. There

Harold Schultz—American Museum of Natural History

Manioc roots are peeled and ground up for flour in this primitive mill.

are farms that produce cotton and mallow for fiber.

A new development is the growing of black pepper and of jute for burlap bags by Japanese immigrants near Santarém. A small textile plant makes the bags for shipping coffee and sugar, as well as for other products. One of the most important things about the jute plantations is that, for the first time, the rich Brazilian floodplains are being used for agriculture.

People from all along the river come to sell their goods and visit on market day in Belém.

Joe Barnell—Shostal

Charles Perry Weimer—House of Photography

One of the earliest settlements in Brazil was at Salvador, now capital and seaport of Bahia State.

The Northeast

The nine states of northeastern Brazil are made up of two very different kinds of land. One, along the east coast, has regular rainfall. The other, to the west, has frequent long droughts and disastrous floods. The soil is too poor for anything but scrubby trees and brush.

The leaves of carnauba palms are gathered for the coating of valuable wax that sticks to them.

Joe Barnell—Shostal

Most of the northeast is highland, with a few lowland areas along the coast. The São Francisco River starts in Minas Gerais and flows through the *sertão* (back country) before it reaches the sea. The São Francisco is not a very useful river for transportation or irrigation. But it does supply a large part of Brazil's electric power.

The first colonists found sugar cane would grow well in the northeast. They cleared the forests around Salvador and Recife and brought in Negro slaves to do the work. The sugar business increased until all the good sugar land was cleared.

At the same time, enormous grants were given by the Portuguese crown for the raising of cattle. Cattlemen became as rich as the sugar planters by the same method, land rotation.

At the beginning of the eighteenth century, gold and diamonds were discovered in Minas Gerais. The name "Minas Gerais" means "general mines." Half a million people left the northeast in a rush to the mines.

Today there are two kinds of sugar mills in the northeast. The biggest are the *usinas,* where modern machinery is used. The smaller mills are called *engenhos.* Here, sugar is made by the old method, boiling the syrup in iron pans over wood fires.

The tobacco fields of Bahía are mostly worked by the descendants of freed Negro slaves. The farms are tiny and the farmers are poor. Every inch of land is used for tobacco.

Except for an area in the south, this is the only place in Brazil today where fertilizer is used regularly. Much of this tobacco is made into cigars in small factories nearby. Skillful women roll them by hand.

Most of the northeastern land is now used for the grazing of cattle and goats, the cattle on the better land, the goats in the poor, dry areas. In such places, the main product is goatskins. Where the cattle graze, the trees must be cleared and grass planted to provide pasture.

The tenant farmers of the drought and flood regions are very poor. They own almost nothing. They move their families often to new places where they hope to make a better living.

The tenants clear the land and plant crops for their own use for a few years. Then they plant grass and move on. The owner is left with cleared pasture for his cattle.

Efforts have been made to save water and control floods, but they have usually failed because of poor planning. Walls built along rivers have crumbled in a rush of flood water. Reservoirs have been built where there was no flat land nearby to irrigate.

The wild plants of the northeast provide tree cotton for soft cord, caroa for fibers to make hammocks, and carnauba wax for shoe polish, floor wax, phonograph records, and lipstick. A valuable oil comes from the nuts of the babaçu palm, but the nuts are collected wastefully.

Cacao is grown along the coast around Bahía on large plantations run by overseers. Workers come from the back country for the harvest.

Many new highways have been built in the northeast, so there has been a great increase in the use of trucks. They go from one town to another exchanging the goods of the whole area. The people here are now for the first time beginning to depend on one another instead of growing and making products for their own use only.

James R. Simon

Paulo Afonso Falls is a tremendous cascade that drops 275 feet and supplies much of Brazil's power.

Charles Perry Weimer—House of Photography

A modern sugar refinery stands in the middle of a large plantation near Recife.

In this dry, seared land of the northeast, there has been no rain for five years.

Birnback

Eastern Brazil and the Central Highlands

The east of Brazil includes the states of São Paulo, Minas Gerais, Espirito Santo, the federal district—Rio de Janeiro—and the vast, almost unoccupied lands behind them, the states of Mato Grosso and Goias.

Eric Pavel—FLO

Volta Redonda is a giant modern steel manufacturing center near Rio de Janeiro.

A beautiful new highway now links Rio de Janeiro and Belo Horizonte, capital of Minas Gerais state.

Joe Barnell—Shostal

Most of the coast is low, with a rainy, tropical climate. The highlands are cooler. In the south it is cloudy and rainy along the coast and there are places where there is frost in winter.

Like most pioneer lands, the history of the Brazilian east is the story of restless people, taking from the land to get rich, wearing it out, then moving on to other places. There has been one kind of wealth after another taken from the land. After each boom, the land has been given over to cattle grazing. Now grass grows where magnificent forests have been. In some places the land is too worn-out to grow even scrub forest.

Minas Gerais is beef and dairy country, mostly made up of large *fazendas* (estates). The *fazenda* workers live isolated on enormous tracts of land or clustered in tiny villages around a church. Their houses are leaky buildings with mud floors and walls.

The early settlements of Minas Gerais were built along roads. Colonial roads were built over the mountains where the forests were thinnest. But later, railroads were built in entirely different places. Level land is best for laying track. Now many of the old settlements are isolated, for the colonial roads have grown over. New all-weather roads are replacing the railroads.

The minerals of Minas Gerais include iron and many other important metals, as well as gemstones. One of the deepest mines in the world still produces gold.

Rio de Janeiro is backed by steep hills cutting the city off from the inland regions.

The iron ore is estimated to be nearly a quarter of the world's supply. A new large-scale steel plant at Volta Redonda processes the iron ore with materials from nearby. But coal for the plant must be imported from West Virginia.

Rio de Janeiro is a magnificent city built on the shores of a perfect natural harbor. It was originally built as a shipping port for the gold from Minas Gerais. It was a good place for defense against Indians and Spaniards because there is a wall of high land behind it. Today Rio is Brazil's center of business and trade. Because of the high land behind it, almost all of Rio de Janeiro's contacts with other parts of Brazil are by sea.

Not all the eastern land is *fazendas* worked by tenant farmers. In the Paraíba Valley, where the floodplain makes good cropland, modern farms have been started. Many people here who had been farming by the old land rotation method have taken up the new ways.

São Paulo state was first settled by adventurers who came seeking quick wealth. When the gold in Minas Gerais was found, people from all over Brazil poured into the east.

At the time the surface gold was used up, coffee became popular in England and North America. Large numbers of people migrated to the land around São Paulo city to plant coffee trees. Soon Brazil was supplying three quarters of the world's coffee. By 1920, Brazil's coffee production had risen tremendously. It was nearly twice what all the countries in the world could use. And new trees were still being planted.

Coffee growers began to lose money, but then a new boom crop developed—cotton. Young coffee trees were pulled up to make room for cotton. Many coffee growers changed over entirely to cotton and new plantations were started by new people.

But during World War II cotton could not be sold to Japan or Europe and many cotton planters turned to oranges. This boom is just starting, but oranges may replace cotton. Already, so little cotton is being grown that Brazilian textile manufacturers are afraid they may have to get it from other countries.

São Paulo has many modern farms. The government has brought in colonists from

A farm in the Paraíba Valley, where new farming methods are being tried on old, worn-out land.

After the coffee beans are harvested, they must be spread in the sun to dry.

The coffee beans are tossed in the air from wire trays to rid them of leaves and dirt.

Japan, Europe, and other parts of Brazil. The farms of the Paraná colonies are on the São Paulo border although they are actually in Paraná state. But the people there are more closely connected with São

Coffee beans must be carefully roasted so as not to spoil their flavor and aroma.

Paulo than with Paraná, because the roads and railroads lead there.

These farms have been very successful. Worn-out land has been enriched. Virgin forest is being preserved. Mixed crops are planted instead of single money crops. Fertilizers and modern machinery are used. The slopes are terraced so the soil will not wash off. The roads and railroads are carefully planned to connect the colonists with the markets for their produce.

But São Paulo's coffee planters still work by the *fazenda* system. The tenant clears the forest and plants coffee trees for the owner. In return, the tenant may plant his own crops between the rows until the trees begin to bear, after four to six years. Then he moves on. The owner harvests coffee until the trees do not produce well any more. Then he moves on, too, and starts all over again on new land.

São Paulo is the richest state in Brazil. Its nine million people produce nearly half of Brazil's coffee, more than half its cotton, and a quarter of its sugar. The city of São Paulo is the biggest manufacturing city in Latin America. The hydroelectric power stations of the state produce three fifths of the power in Brazil.

H. Wilhelmy

The houses of the German colonists in southern Brazil are solid and permanent.

Forest land has been devastated so that coffee trees can be planted on a Brazilian plantation.

John and Bini Moss—Photo Researchers

Southern Brazil

The south of Brazil is made up of three states: Paraná, Santa Catarina and Rio Grande do Sul. The land along the coast is mostly lowland and part of the Great Escarpment. Back of this are hills and a few high mountains. Next, to the west, is lowland, and furthest inland is the Paraná Plateau.

This is one of the world's largest lava plateaus. The rivers that cross it have cut deep canyons. At the heads of the canyons are spectacular waterfalls where the water drops several hundred feet.

Most of the area has a plentiful rainfall all year. In the north are thick forests of tropical trees. To the south, the trees become thinner and the land is covered with grass. The cool highlands are covered with dense pine forests. The minerals of this section are mainly copper and iron ore, and there are low-grade coal deposits.

The people of the south are European, but not of Portuguese descent. They are German, Italian, Swiss, Austrian, and in Paraná, Polish and Russian. The way most of them live is not like most of Brazil's people.

These European settlers have always known that there was no source of quick wealth here. They are interested in establishing permanent homes and villages. They grow crops on fertilized land year after year. They have built strong houses

In contrast to the modern, progressive parts of Brazil is the little-known, vast highland country of Mato Grosso and Goias. Only seven out of a hundred of Brazil's people live here, although it is two thirds of Brazil's land. There are some successful farms, near roads to market. There is much land that has been turned back to cattle grazing by farmers who were unable to get their produce to market.

Near Corumbá is iron ore and manganese. Workers have been drawn to the mines here. They are prosperous enough so that many people use Corumbá's airfield. Planes come to it from all over the country.

In this enormous, almost empty, stretch of land is the exact center of Brazil. The new capital, Brasilia, has been built here. Unlike most cities, Brasilia was completely finished before it was occupied. It is designed for half a million government workers and the people who will supply them with goods and services. The government hopes that settlers will be drawn to the land around the city to clear forests and grow food for the city.

Hopeful prospectors pan for gold and diamonds in the shallow upper Paraguay River in Mato Grosso.

This has been tried once before in Brazil. The state of Minas Gerais built a similar new capital, Belo Horizonte. But after fifty years, there are still almost no farms around this beautiful city and food is still brought from far away. The only new people to come have moved into the city.

Brasilia, the new capital of Brazil, was completely finished before anyone moved into its buildings.

On the open prairies of Brazil's far south are great livestock ranches like those of Argentina.

Southern Brazil grows large quantities of rice. Here, a machine does the hard work of threshing.

and they raise many children. Their settlements keep growing.

Some of the first settlers who went to the south were Germans. They were brought in by the Brazilian government to protect this almost empty land from the invading Spaniards. They stayed, building typical German communities and planting German crops such as rye and potatoes, as well as Brazilian crops such as corn.

Later, Italians came. They built typical Italian villages surrounded by vineyards. These communities expanded. Soon all the big estates which had been granted to Portuguese settlers were divided into small farms. The new colonists were able to set up a democratic government because there was no owner-tenant system.

When Brazil first started settling the south, the government made the mistake of placing the colonists in isolated places. But it soon found that where there were no roads or railroads, the communities failed. The farmers could not reach markets and they gradually turned back to the old land rotation system.

The new wheat-growing settlements in Paraná state are established around a road system built when the people were first settled. These settlements have prospered from the beginning.

The main areas where there are still large estates are the open plains. Here gauchos roam with cattle and sheep. And in the Jacquí River Valley people of Portuguese descent grow rice for large owners. In the cattle country the main products are hides, wool and salt beef. The beef is processed in large factories in Pelotas.

An Italian colony in Santa Catarina grows rice and tobacco, but its biggest products are pork, lard, milk, and butter. Cattle are kept in barns where the manure can be saved for fertilizer.

In western Paraná the forests contain stands of maté (Paraguayan tea). In Porto Alegre there are numerous factories. This city has many road and railroad connections with the rest of the country.

Pôrto Alegre, chief city of the far south, specializes in food-processing industries and tanning.

COUNTRIES OF THE INTERIOR

Bolivia and Paraguay, the two countries of the interior, have many things in common. The most important of these is that neither country has a seacoast. To get to a seaport, they must cross the territory of other countries.

They are isolated not only by political boundaries, but also by natural barriers. In order to get its products to a port, Bolivia must send them over the Andes to the Pacific coast, a very expensive undertaking. It cannot send them down the Amazon to the Atlantic, because the Bolivian rivers which drain into the Amazon are not navigable.

Paraguay, far in the interior of the continent, is isolated by swamps and low areas which are flooded during much of the year. Its chief connection with the outside world is the Paraná-Paraguay system.

Lake Titicaca is one of the few dependable sources of water for farming in the Bolivian highlands.

Ewing Krainin—Photo Researchers

These rivers are shallow, twisting, and full of snags, shoals, and sandbars. The course is constantly changing, so the pilots of the riverboats must always be on their guard against running aground. The rivers sometimes shift so much that settlements along their banks are left miles away from them. They are so winding that a boat must sail many miles along the river to progress a few miles as the crow flies.

Since we know that most of the traffic between the great population centers of South America goes by boat, we can see what the lack of access to the coast means to these countries of the interior. They are unable to get most of their products to a market, and so have remained poor.

Because travel is so difficult, they have had little contact with the people of other countries (except for war), and few new ideas have come in. Life has gone on in the old, traditional way, with few changes.

Another thing that Bolivia and Paraguay have in common is that so many of the people have Indian blood. Three out of every six Bolivians are pure-blooded Indians, and two more are mestizos. Practically all the Paraguayans are mestizos, and Guaraní, an Indian language, is spoken by most of the people.

Both Bolivia and Paraguay have suffered terribly from wars. In the war between Chile, Peru, and Bolivia in 1879-1883, Bolivia lost its only seaport and the valuable nitrate beds.

Paraguay also fought a very long and costly war, against Brazil, Argentina, and Uruguay. The war lasted five years, from 1865 to 1870. When it was over, Paraguay's population had shrunk from 1,300,000 to 250,000. Only about 29,000 of the survivors were men!

Both countries took a long time to recover from their losses. But in 1932 they went to war with each other over the for-

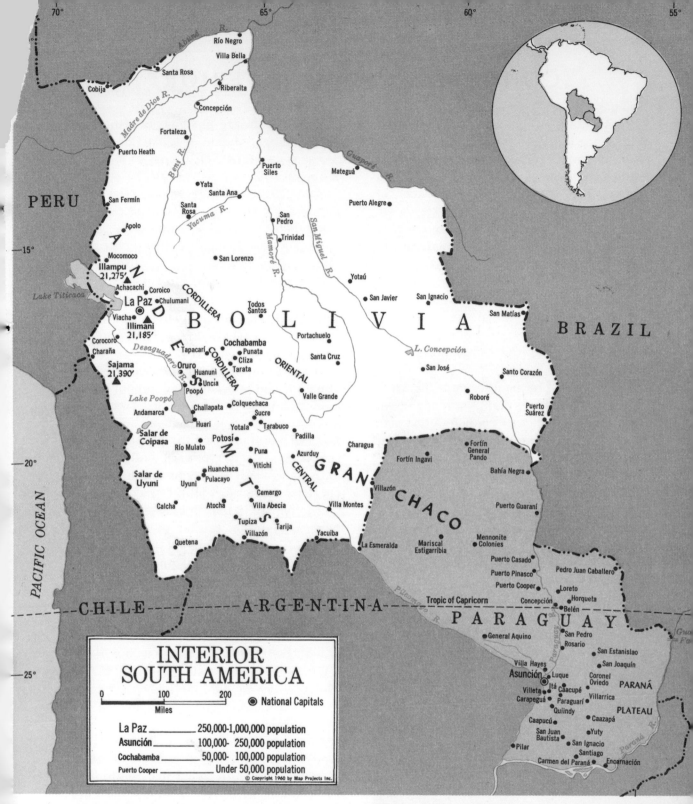

INTERIOR
SOUTH AMERICA

0	100	200

Miles

◉ National Capitals

La Paz _____ 250,000-1,000,000 population
Asunción _____ 100,000- 250,000 population
Cochabamba _____ 50,000- 100,000 population
Puerto Cooper _____ Under 50,000 population

© Copyright 1960 by Map Projects Inc.

ested lowland called the Gran Chaco, of which both countries claimed a part.

Bolivia wanted the Chaco because of the Paraguay River. Bolivia's leaders thought (mistakenly) the river would provide a route to the Atlantic and the great ports of Buenos Aires and Montevideo. Paraguay's leaders coveted the Chaco because there was oil in the Bolivian part. When both sides had fought until they were completely exhausted, Bolivia still had no route to the sea and Paraguay still had no oil.

Bolivia

Bolivia is a large country, but only a small portion of its territory is used. Its total area is 424,000 square miles, about as large as Texas and California combined, but most of the 3,235,000 people live in an area the size of Connecticut.

Although practically all of Bolivia's income comes from mining, only about four per cent of the people are miners. Most Bolivians make a bare living from farming and herding.

Kofod—Monkmeyer

Bolivian Indians plant potatoes by the shore of Lake Titicaca. In background is a reed canoe.

Steep slopes and rocky soils of the Bolivian Andes make farming difficult and crop yields low.

Tom Hollyman—Photo Researchers

The western third of Bolivia lies high in the Andes. It is a dry, cold region. The eastern two thirds are a warm, moist lowland. Most of the people live in the mountains and the *Altiplano,* a high, bleak plateau between the eastern and western ranges of the Andes.

The Altiplano is over 12,000 feet above sea level. La Paz, the chief city and seat of Bolivia's government, is located at the bottom of a 1,400-foot canyon in the Altiplano. The mountains are so steep, high, and rugged that it is almost impossible to reach the eastern lowlands from the highlands. And the communities of the mountain basins are isolated from each other by the towering peaks and ridges.

In the region around Lake Titicaca there is enough rain to grow crops without irrigation. The lake is very large—120 miles long. In some places it is 700 feet deep. Here the Aymaras, an Indian people, raise potatoes and grain and herd llamas.

In the dry area south of Lake Titicaca, the settlements are located at the base of the mountains, where streams provide water for irrigation.

The main farming region of Bolivia is in the warm, well-watered valleys of the eastern chain of mountains. Here the people are mostly mestizo or European. Where the valleys are narrow, farms follow the streams like ribbons for miles. Grains are grown, and fruits do well on the lower slopes. The farm produce is sold to the mining towns of the highlands. Sucre, the official capital of Bolivia, is located in one of these basins.

There are few settlers in the *yungas*— the rainy, forest-covered eastern slopes of the Andes. There is some gold mining. A few planters raise cacao, sugar and coca bushes, the leaves of which are chewed by the highland Indians. Some wild rubber is gathered in the forests and cattle are grazed on the wet savannas.

The southeast of Bolivia is relatively dry. Here the vegetation is scrub forest and

Bolivian miners live in squalid towns in the barren, bleak highlands near the mines.

This Bolivian miner of Potosí must wear heavy clothing against the cold of the 14,000-foot height.

grassland. Before World War I, the region was mostly used for cattle-grazing on large ranches, with some farming.

But oil was discovered in 1920 and this isolated region became important. After the Chaco War with Paraguay, the Bolivian government strengthened the connections between the Chaco and the population centers of the highlands. Pipelines were constructed to refineries at Cochabamba and Sucre. A highway between Santa Cruz, the chief town of the Chaco, and Cochabamba was completed in 1953.

The government is also trying to increase the population and food production by offering land to settlers. Although there is probably more oil to be discovered, Bolivia cannot afford the cost of exploring for new wells.

The mountains of Bolivia are rich in metals. The copper mine at Corocoro has been worked since Inca times. It is one of the two sources of pure copper in the Western Hemisphere.

Another mining center is Potosí, 14,000 feet high. The mountain which towers 2,000 feet over the town at its base is a rich ore body containing tin, silver, bismuth, and tungsten. But temperatures are very low here because of the altitude. Fuel is

hard to get, and the thin air makes work exhausting.

The mines at Oruro and Uncia are more important today. Though their ores are not as rich as those of Potosí, they are easier to work. These mines produce mostly tin. Other metals of the highlands include lead, zinc, and gold.

Most of Bolivia's tin production was formerly controlled by three large corporations. But in 1952 the government took over control of the mines. One of Bolivia's most serious problems is that the country depends on one product—tin—for over half its income. If the tin market is bad, poverty becomes worse than ever.

Oil wells and storage tanks make a strange scene in the jungle of the Bolivian Chaco.

Paraguay

Paraguay is about the size of California. The eastern third of the country is a rolling plateau from one to two thousand feet high. The rest is level lowland.

The Paraguay River, bordered by great swamps, flows through the center of the country. West of the Paraguay River is the Chaco. The east is covered with forests of tall trees, some of them evergreen. As the climate becomes drier toward the west, the trees thin out and become smaller, but there are thick forests along the streams.

Paraguay has the possibilities of being a rich agricultural land like Uruguay. The climate is moderate. There is enough rain for farming. The soil is rich. But in spite of these advantages, Paraguay is the poorest country in all South America.

Most of the people are tenant farmers, producing crops for their own use on rented land. There are about 1,650,000 people in Paraguay, most of whom live in the hills between the plateau and the east bank of the Paraguay River. Here the land is high enough to escape flooding, and the people are near the country's main route of transportation. Asunción, the capital, is located at a spot where the high ground touches the river.

Paraguay's chief commercial crop is cotton. Other crops are corn, manioc, sweet potatoes, rice, sugar cane, and tobacco.

Another important product is quebracho extract from the quebracho trees which grow along the west bank of the Paraguay River. This extract is used in tanning leather. Maté is both cultivated and gathered. The eastern forests yield lumber.

Another export is petitgrain oil, distilled from bitter oranges. This oil is used in perfumes, and Paraguay produces seven tenths of the world's supply. Cattle are raised in the central part of the country, and their hides and meat are exported.

The government is trying to increase food production by offering the people new farmland, but most of the people are too poor to buy the land, even at low prices.

Guaraní Indian huts near Asunción. The Guaranís were the original inhabitants of Paraguay.

J. D. Winbray—Shostal

The imposing Presidential Palace in Asunción overlooks the Paraguay River.

Davis Pratt—Rapho Guillumette

Julien Bryan—Photo Researchers

The grasslands of central Paraguay provide pasture for herds of beef cattle.

Eric Pavel—FLO

The faces of this Paraguayan farm couple examining the cotton crop show a lifetime of hard work.

Paraguay has deposits of iron, copper, and manganese, but these have been very little exploited. Most of Paraguay's industries are connected with the processing of food products.

The war with Argentina, Brazil, and Uruguay set Paraguay back severely. Some European settlers immigrated after the war and helped to revive the country, but it remained very poor.

Until the twentieth century, the river was the only connection between Asunción and the outside world. In 1913 a railroad was completed from Buenos Aires to Asunción, but it did not end Paraguay's isolation.

The trains had to cross the river twice on ferries. The volume of traffic was so low that the railroad had to charge very high rates. Even today it costs as much to send goods from Buenos Aires to Asunción by rail as it does to send the same goods by ship to Japan.

But the airplane has brought many changes. Asunción is a center of air travel, with connections with all the neighboring countries.

A ferry across the Paraguay River and a connecting road link Asunción to Argen-

Davis Pratt—Rapho Guillumette

Oxcarts are a more common mode of transportation than trains in Paraguay.

tina's road system, and roads have been planned to connect with Brazil's highways.

Santos, Brazil's chief port, has been declared an open port through which goods may go to Paraguay duty-free. Now Paraguay can bring in goods more cheaply.

If the road connections with Brazil are actually built, Paraguay will have its first surface connection with the outside world that does not go through Argentina.

THE FUTURE OF SOUTH AMERICA

As a whole, South America is just beginning to enter the modern age. True, there are many places that are just as advanced as the same kinds of places on other continents. South America has some of the most modern cities in the world. Belo Horizonte and Brasilia are unique. Probably nowhere else have big cities been entirely built before any of the inhabitants moved in. But this only emphasizes the undeveloped state of most of the continent.

Eric Hess—Triangle

An American-made bulldozer clears the jungle near Belém, Brazil, for a new farming development.

Many of South America's steel plants, power plants, and factories are as up-to-date as any in the world. Some of the farming areas have started as virgin forest and become model agricultural communities.

Only a continent with the history of South America could make these great changes so suddenly and completely. It is the story of a land that has almost stood still for several centuries.

The settlement of South America started a hundred years before the first handful of settlers came to North America. But "settlement" is not an accurate word for what the

South American explorers had in mind when they arrived.

They did not want to settle down on one piece of land and build homes for their families. They wanted to roam over the continent seeking wealth.

If they had to be content with land instead of gold, they wanted enormous amounts of land. Large estates would make them important in the eyes of their countrymen. There was plenty of land for everyone who came. And there were many Indians on much of it to produce paying crops. The continent seemed endless.

When the land they first used was worn out, there was always the land across the valley for the next crop. This was the attitude of the first explorers, and they handed it down to their descendants.

In a few places, successful colonies were started by people who knew from the beginning that there was no great wealth on the land they occupied. They worked hard, raised children, and became moderately prosperous. Their children grew up with the idea that the farms were their homes —not just a source of money.

But communities like these have been started only recently and have been very few in South America. So it is almost as if

Below is one of the modern government buildings of Brasilia, the new capital of Brazil.

Richard Davis—House of Photography

Charles Perry Weimer—House of Photography

Greater development of irrigation will mean increased food production and better living.

the real settlement of South America started at the beginning of this century. There are many problems to solve, but there are better ways of solving them than ever before. South America has always been called part of the New World, but it is just beginning to be new as Old World methods disappear.

There is room for many more people in South America. It is a very thinly populated continent, especially the vast interior regions. Some parts of the interior have never been explored. And there will be many more people in South America. It is estimated that by the end of this century, the population will be three times larger.

Naturally, when there are more people, they will need more land. And there is an almost endless amount of land on the continent. Some of it, of course, is poor land. But we have seen that even deserts can produce food when they are irrigated. Much of it is good land, but it is so far from roads that it cannot be used.

Many of the governments of South American countries have learned about the best ways to establish colonies in the great empty land. They know there must be roads and railroads. There must be airports.

Then the colonists will be able to sell what they produce to other colonists and to cities. When they sell their own products, they earn money. With the money they will be able to buy the goods of other people and everyone will prosper.

Prosperous, contented people do not wander over the land, using it up and moving on. They stay in communities. These centers become cities.

Farming in the twentieth century does not take as many people as it did several centuries ago, and as it still does in most of South America. The new communities will practice modern farming. Governments will probably help colonists to buy machinery. The colonists will learn about flood control and irrigation, about fertilizers, and how to breed animals scientifically.

Great changes will take place. Since machinery will not work on steep slopes, the mountainsides will be used for tree crops such as coffee and oranges. Forests will be

New hydroelectric projects will help overcome the power shortage caused by lack of coal.

Joe Barnell—Shostal

allowed to grow back on other slopes to hold the soil and provide timber. Crops will be grown on the land best suited for each kind, and more food will be produced.

The system by which the farmer grows only enough to feed himself and his family will disappear. Instead, one farmer will grow enough to feed twenty people. One man on a tractor can do the work of many men with hoes.

Many people will move to the cities to work in industries. Industries will grow because there will be more paid workers. And workers who earn good wages are able to buy the goods their industries produce.

The prosperous farmers and the industrial workers will create a class of people that is lacking in South America—a class which any country must have if its people are to prosper. These people who will have a moderate amount of money will become South America's new middle class.

There is already a wealthy class and there is a vast number of very poor people. As President Batlle y Ordóñez of Uruguay said, ". . . the poor should be made less poor." When the poor have jobs and farms, they will be less poor. And when the standard of living is raised for any of them, it will be raised a little for all of them.

More children are receiving an education. This will help South America break free from the past.

Ernst Baumann—Birnback

Industries will need raw materials and power. South America has so many different climates that almost anything can be grown somewhere on the continent. It already produces enormous amounts of corn and wheat, sugar and coffee, cotton and wool, cacao and tobacco. Its herds of sheep and cattle are tremendous. Many other crops could be grown in greater quantities than they are, with good planning.

South America has great mineral reserves. Its copper and tin and oil supplies seem never to grow smaller. It has iron ore and bauxite, manganese and tungsten. It has precious metals—gold, silver, and platinum—and gem stones.

It is true that there is very little coal. But more may be found when the continent is more thickly settled. Or it may still be necessary to import it from other places. There is no continent in the world that can supply all its own industrial needs.

South America has many spectacular waterfalls with which to make power, but many of them are far from where the power is needed. Perhaps the answer will be to build the industries where the power is. Or perhaps nuclear power will be the answer.

Industries need educated workers. All the South American republics have free primary schools. Most of the countries have laws that say all children must go to school until they are thirteen or fourteen. Most of the countries have high schools and vocational schools and universities. But still there are many adults and children who are unable to read and write. Undoubtedly there are people who live too far from schools to send their children to them.

Transportation is the answer to many of these problems, just as lack of transportation has been the reason many of them were not solved long ago.

Roads will help to fill the empty land and to make settlers prosperous in new colonies. Roads will be necessary for modern farming, to make it possible to use the best land even when it is far from markets.

Roads will help industries to import raw materials and to ship products to other places. Roads will make mines and oil land easier to reach. Roads will make it possible to carry equipment to places where power plants can be built. Roads will make it possible for children to go to school.

Roads will connect isolated settlements to one another. When men can reach each other, they will exchange goods and ideas. They will prosper and learn about how other people live.

Small communities will join together and become larger communities. People who are isolated from the world, struggling to make a bare living for themselves, will be drawn into industry or modern mines and farms.

When this happens, South America will be using its greatest natural resource, its isolated people who have so far taken no part in the agriculture, industry, trade—or prosperity—of their countries.

Roy Pinney—Photo Library

Above, this muddy stretch of road under construction is part of the Pan-American Highway.

Caracas, Venezuela, with its clean, modern buildings, shows what the future may bring.

Leo Matiz—Pix

SOUTH AMERICA—FACTS AND FIGURES

COUNTRIES: AREA AND POPULATION

Country	Area in sq. miles	Population (est. 1960)
Argentina	1,084,100	20,882,200
Bolivia	421,400	3,570,800
Brazil	3,287,700	65,979,400
Chile	286,400	7,582,500
Colombia	439,600	14,244,000
Ecuador	106,200	4,185,400
Guiana, British	83,000	576,200
Guiana, French	34,800	32,000
Paraguay	157,000	1,789,900
Peru	510,000	10,686,000
Surinam (Dutch Guiana)	55,100	287,600
Uruguay	72,200	2,776,500
Venezuela	352,100	6,602,400

LARGE CITIES AND THEIR POPULATION

City and Country (or State)	Population (est. 1960)
Buenos Aires, Argentina	3,750,000
São Paulo, Brazil	3,149,504
Rio de Janeiro, Brazil	2,940,045
Santiago, Chile	1,627,962
Caracas, Venezuela	1,189,000
Lima, Peru	1,186,000
Bogotá, Colombia	1,044,760
Montevideo, Uruguay	950,000
Recife, Brazil	703,726
Medellín, Colombia	545,860
Salvador, Brazil	532,619
Pôrto Alegre, Brazil	512,951
Belo Horizonte, Brazil	501,428
Rosario, Argentina	467,937
Córdoba, Argentina	450,091
Maracaibo, Venezuela	423,000
Barranquilla, Colombia	392,330
Guayaquil, Ecuador	350,000
La Paz, Bolivia	321,045

HIGHEST MOUNTAINS AND THEIR ELEVATIONS

Mountain and Country	Height in feet
Aconcagua, Argentina	22,835
Ojos del Salado, Argentina-Chile	22,550
Tupungato, Argentina-Chile	22,310
Huascarán, Peru	22,205
Tocorpuri, Chile-Bolivia	22,162
Llullaillaco, Argentina-Chile	22,100
Mercedario, Argentina	21,885
Yerupaja, Peru	21,760
Incahuasi, Argentina-Chile	21,700
Tres Cruces, Argentina-Chile	21,700
Illampú, Bolivia	21,490
Sajama, Bolivia	21,390
Nacimiento, Argentina	21,300
Illimani, Bolivia	21,185
Antofalla, Argentina	21,100
Chimborazo, Ecuador	20,580

LARGEST LAKES AND THEIR AREAS

Lake and Country	Area in sq. miles
Maracaibo, Venezuela	6,300
Titicaca, Bolivia-Peru	3,200
Poopó, Bolivia	970
Buenos Aires, Argentina	865
Argentino, Argentina	546
Mar Chiquita, Argentina	450
Viedma, Argentina	420
Colhué, Argentina	310
Llanquihue, Chile	300
Nahuel Huapí, Argentina	210

LONGEST RIVERS AND THEIR LENGTH

River and Region of South America	Length in miles
Amazon, Andes-Brazil	3,900
Madeira, Interior-Brazil	2,100
Paraná, Brazil-Interior	2,050
São Francisco, Brazil	1,800
Orinoco, Northern	1,700
Tocantins, Brazil	1,640
Araguaia, Brazil	1,630
Pilcomayo, Interior	1,550
Negro, Brazil	1,400
Paraguay, Interior	1,300
Juruá, Brazil	1,250
Tapajóz, Brazil	1,250
Xingú, Brazil	1,230
Magdalena, Northern	1,000
Uruguay, Brazil-Southern	1,000